Quality Time

Easing
The Children
Through Divorce

· · ·

Quality Time

· · ·

MELVIN G. GOLDZBAND, M.D.

MCGRAW-HILL BOOK COMPANY
New York · St. Louis · San Francisco · Auckland · Bogotá
Guatemala · Hamburg · Johannesburg · Lisbon · London
Madrid · Mexico · Montreal · New Delhi · Panama · Paris
San Juan · São Paulo · Singapore · Sydney
Tokyo · Toronto

Dedication

· · ·

To all the kids and their parents, struggling to
do the right thing in the eye of the tornado . . .

123456789 DOCDOC 8765

ISBN 0-07-023693-3

LIBRARY OF CONGRESS CATALOGING IN PUBLICATION DATA

Goldzband, Melvin G.
   Quality time.

   1. Children of divorced parents—United States.
2. Divorce—United States. I. Title.
HQ777.5.G65   1985   646.7′8   84-26167
ISBN 0-07-023693-3

Book Design by Mary A. Wirth

WE

Table of Contents

--------------- . . . ---------------

Preface

Most parents do not sit up nights planning how to mess up their children's lives. Rather, most parents are caring individuals who rightly consider themselves responsible for doing the best they can for their children, even during times of extraordinary stress. Divorce is one of those times.

Sometimes, in the midst of the divorce battle, with the struggle to maintain one's own identity and purpose in life, parents unwittingly and unwillingly do harmful things to their children. Divorcing the children's other parent may even be the first of these, although the divorce may be necessary for the parents to maintain their integrity and self-respect. However, following the parents' separation, the children will be much more vulnerable than they would have been if the parents had stayed together.

Don't get me wrong—*everything about divorce does not have to affect the children negatively,* but, in the midst of the struggle, parents sometimes act in unthinking ways. They may be carried away by their own insecurity about the divorce or by their feelings toward their spouse, and they can do a great deal of harm to the children. Some of the harm can be undone, but it is better left undone in the first place. I hope that this book will help prevent some of that harm.

Divorcing parents need to recognize what they are doing to themselves as well as to their children when they battle over the kids. If you are a divorcing parent, you may endanger your own relationships with your kids when you fight over them. Of course, divorcing parents also need to learn that the effects of these battles on the children are horrendous, although long and sad experience shows that these effects may not be evident until later.

In this book, I repeatedly point out that divorcing parents operate in the eye of an emotional tornado and that they really cannot be expected to function rationally all the time, much less to think clearly and logically. This is why this book can be very valuable. It is always there, even at the worst of times. It is always available to refer to, to remind you of the harm that could be done to all concerned, including yourself, and to suggest alternatives. It can be picked up at odd hours and at quiet times, when reading can bring greater understanding and, I hope, can prevent possibly harmful events.

Many examples of situations between you and your spouse will come to your mind as you read this book, and you may find that they are not in the text. Insert those examples from your own experience into the appropriate spots and think about the effects of those examples as well as the ones already in the book. You write the book, too! Thus, you will develop more ideas and concepts about the varied situations affecting the children of divorce and their parents, and you will see them from a number of points of view.

You are not meant to answer the questions at the end of most of the sections easily or quickly. In fact, many may have no real right or wrong answers. I asked these questions in the same way that I question parents who come to see me in my office. Sometimes the questions may make you angry or upset—this means that they hit you where you live and that a problem area may have been nudged. In that case, you should think about the questions and your answers even harder. You may find that you will make some different decisions based on some new and different ideas.

If you begin to consider situations and examples which are not in the book, see if they can be related to those in the book. See if you can fit them appropriately to some of the questions, too. Even better, try to ask yourselves even more pointed questions about your own examples, similar to those asked in the book. A good psychiatrist wants patients to start questioning themselves about feelings and reasons for troublesome behavior or feelings, so save yourself some time and money by working hard on the questions. But, if you need to see someone, don't hesitate—you may help not only yourself but your kids as well. After all, who needs anxious parents?

Acknowledgments

Maintaining a private practice and a family life while attempting to write coherently is a juggling act. It requires a good family. I'm lucky. I appreciate that my wife maintained her good humor most of the time. If parents who are divorcing could do that as well, their children would benefit! My trusty computer, my *Eagle II*, with its excellent word processing program, also helped me enormously. It is a great creative tool. However, I have not yet figured out how such a machine–or any machine–can directly help divorcing parents. I wish a machine could do that. But as yet, it's strictly a human endeavor, and sometimes a very tough one. I hope this book helps.

I owe special thanks to the Honorable Elizabeth Nay Zumwalt, of the Superior Court of California, in San Diego County. She took special interest in this book; it was she who suggested that questions might help readers to delve a little more deeply into their own feelings and situations. I am especially grateful to her for that. I am also grateful to many other family law judges throughout the United States and Canada and to countless matrimonial lawyers and child protective workers in both countries. They provided encouragement, help, and support in my attempts to develop new methods of dealing with this ugliest of litigations.

Melvin G. Goldzband, M.D., F.A.P.A.
San Diego, California
October 1st, 1984

CHAPTER 1

· · ·

Rationalizations and Realities

If only very young kids could talk—*really talk* or *really write* as, say, Winston Churchill or even Bill Moyers does. If only they could discuss events and relationships and feelings from their own points of view. As the media flacks would say, if only they could *conceptualize*! However, since they can't, we adults must verbalize and write about what we wish the kids could tell us. "Quality time" is a terrific example of such an adult phrase used to describe worthwhile activities shared between child and parent when their time together is restricted by separation or divorce. It is a really good phrase, and the concept it represents is even better. If parents separate or divorce and one parent is not able to be with his or her children as frequently or as routinely as before, then the time spent with those kids is even more valuable to all of them than it was before the divorce. At least it should be, and parents and children should recognize that it is very precious time.

Adults and children often define quality time differently. Frequently, children do not perceive that the time their visiting parents spend with them is of such high quality, regardless of what their parents might call it. Psychiatrists know that to be true because psychiatrists listen to some kids when they are very young, to more kids when they are older, and to lots of adults who let us know in retrospect what they felt or thought as small children. By then it may be too late to undo the problems of childhood. But the sharing of those feelings and experiences will allow us to do better with our own kids, as all of us want to do. When they separate or divorce, most parents want to make the inevitable trauma of their breakup as easy as possible for their children. This trauma cannot be eliminated; it can be reduced.

Children always suffer more from their parents' divorce than do their parents, and it is likely (but definitely not inevitable) that smaller children suffer more than older children. But parents can learn much about themselves and their attitudes about their children. They can learn that the attitudes they think they have may not be the attitudes that they demonstrate in their relationships with their children. Also, they can discover, if they are motivated, that their activities with their children during their newly limited times might not be as high quality as they believe. Parents can also learn to turn the time they spend with their children into genuine quality time. The kids will do better for it, and so will the parents.

Sometimes we adults kid ourselves. As parents, we like to think we are learning about our children's lives and their needs, but sometimes we blithely ignore those same needs and proceed on our own self-serving ways, especially in times of stress when we may not be able to give as much to our children. Most adults do not sit up nights, planning to destroy their children by ignoring their needs. When adults do not do their best by their kids, it is rarely because they don't want to; rather, they simply do not recognize what they are doing. Stressful times allow us to recognize even less than we do during other times, and separation and divorce are among the most stressful of times.

Kids, of course, see differently than do grown-ups. In their terms, the best time is spent with parents who really care about them, who demonstrate real and continued interest in them and in their activities, and, most important, who are really dependable. If they could conceive of such things in such terms, very young children might well define one very good example of quality time as those few moments spent by a parent holding his or her child's head over the toilet bowl while the child is throwing up into it. No one is more dependent than a small child. The human infant is born into this world more helpless for a longer time than the newborn of any other species. By and large, that is the main reason that the breaking up of a family is so disastrous for young children. They fear that no one will take care of them, and their fear is realistic. They are overtly dependent creatures, and they simply cannot get along in this world without the presence of strong, dependable adults who really care for them.

Divorce is so common in U.S. society these days that it affects vast numbers of children. Children always have trouble coping with divorce, but the troubles get far worse when the adults who should continue to demonstrate their dependability fail to do so. Practically all adults want to continue being parents to their own children, with everything that the term and the status of parenthood entails. But often, when times are emotionally hard for them, such as in the middle of a hard-fought and bitter separation, they may have little left to give to the children who need them even more then. This is the danger point. This book is aimed at parents of both sexes whose lives have been shattered by their own divorces—or are being shattered now—to alert them to what they are doing to their kids and to what they might do to make things a little better for their children and for themselves.

Escaping into a Cliché

Perhaps you are already familiar with the term "quality time." The example I gave of holding the young child's head might not mesh with the definition you might give. Many parents, when questioned about the phrase, automatically think of sharing an intellectual or some other type of striving activity with the child, as if quality were defined only as representative of cultural enhancement. Many parents describe reading classics to their children or getting books for them in the local library as quality time. Certainly, it may well be, but quality is as quality does.

Remember, the example—extreme as it may be—represents the young child's point of view, and in this book very little else counts. These days, many people toss off the phrase "quality time" easily and meaninglessly. This is a dangerous trend among many parents who may not be as conscientious as they believe they are. Most adults who abuse the phrase are divorced parents who do not have custody of their children, and they abuse the term by using it to refer to the abbreviated time they spend with their children; the term often becomes part of a rationalization for not devoting sufficient time or energy to them. These parents make themselves feel better by saying, "Of course, I really can't spend very much time with Junior, but when I do, I make sure that it's quality time!" It then becomes a cliché.

The idea of sharing genuine quality time with children needs no defense. In contrast, the conscious and unconscious reasons why some parents make phony productions of the times they spend with their children need explanations, and they provide the basis for this book. Whether or not they recognize it, those parents feel guilt someplace within themselves over what they did to their children in breaking up the family. They feel a need to make up to them. If they recognize that they can never really make up to them, then they often kid themselves, their children, and the world that they are at least trying. That self-kidding is dangerous for both parent and child. It leaves them both out in the emotional cold.

No one has ever developed the officially approved dictionary definition of quality time. I doubt very strongly that the people who use the term so glibly to kid themselves consider the children's view in defining it. Certainly, they do not define it as the children might. I doubt that the parents even consider how much high quality is associated with lovingly taking care of a sick child. The kids sure know it and appreciate it, at least as far as kids can appreciate anything at tender ages. They tell us later that they did—and do.

———— · ————

Quality time provides mainly for the needs of the child and demonstrates without question to the child that the parent is concerned about those very needs. As such, it gratifies both child and giving parent. Kids remember, and so do adults.

———— · ————

Occasionally or hurriedly visiting parents define quality time in their own individual ways to suit their own purposes and capacities. Many of those parents feel quite guilt-ridden, not only over their postdivorce relationships with their children, but also over the divorce itself. It is not hard to see how clutching at the term, taking refuge in it, and beating it to death by overuse can provide solace for those guilt feelings. Often, those parents genuinely feel that they are doing the best they can with and for their children. Often they are right. More often, they are not.

Disneyland Parents

Another term describes a different kind of visiting parent—the "Disneyland parent." This has developed into an even newer cliché. Just like those who cling to the concept of quality time as a rationalization, Disneyland parents generally are divorced parents of either sex who, for the most part, do not have custody of their children. When they visit their children they do little with them other than provide them with the type of passive amusement characteristic of a carnival or a movie. The phrase has a definite, negative connotation, of course, which is grossly unfair to that marvelous place. Probably such parents consider their amusement park experiences with their children as quality time. Certainly, it may be.

Obviously, providing a good time for a child can be a quality experience for both child and providing parent. Often, though, parents neglect to provide any personal or active experience of their own for children. All the classic Disneyland parent ever does is take children to a place of amusement where the children amuse themselves while the parent usually watches. Sometimes, the parent actually reads or does something else solitary while the children wander off, promising to return in a couple of hours so that the visiting parent will not return them too late to the parent at home. Late returns, of course, spark rows between the estranged parents, as everything seems to do with some estranged parents or even with some still remaining together. Children know that they have had enough of these and do not want to provoke any more.

It takes little imagination to realize how terribly strained the visitation time spent with a Disneyland parent must be for both child and parent. The child wants and needs so very much more from the parent, probably continually tries to get it, and is usually crushed in the bargain. Repetition of this type of visitation causes the child to perceive the visiting parent as a person with whom no deep, meaningful, or helpful relationship can develop. These children then become discouraged and depressed and most likely begin to feel simply unloveable. Try that self-image throughout life!

How can a parent avoid being a Disneyland parent? What can parents do to ensure that time spent with their children is really quality time? So often I hear single parents, especially single fathers, complain to me that they feel an almost total inability to communicate with their children. In such cases, important distinctions must be made. Is the problem really one of *inability* to communicate? If so, is the inability to communicate only restricted to the relationship between parent and child? If the problem is a general one for the parent, treatment for it may be necessary because this may represent a basic personality problem.

Communication problems are not rare. Many people find it very difficult to relate to others, even on the most superficial basis. Sometimes the most superficial basis is all that can be achieved. When that level is all that can be achieved between parent and child, the child suffers—and, as my patients tell me, so do the frustrated parents. They want to go deeper with the kids, but they cannot.

I have made a number of suggestions to those parents, some of which actually work! My goal is to create a basis for the visitation in which the parent learns about the child and participates in the child's life, instead of making the visitation a special, carnival event in the life of the child. The visiting parent probably has little enough time with the child and little enough contact with the child's activities. When the visiting parent uses time to engage in the child's routine activities, whether in school, in scouting, in Little League, in music lessons, or in other activities, the parent learns a great deal about the son or daughter, and these activities provide the basis for communication which might otherwise be difficult.

The parent should ask the child about the child's activities, and if it is at all possible, the parent should participate in some of those activities. Sometimes children will shrug off their activities and will not want to discuss them, but, if visiting parents persist, especially if they express a wish to work with the children in some activities, children will usually respond. If the child has a school project for a special class, the visiting parent should help. If there is a camp-out with the scouts, the visiting parent should participate. If the child has music lessons on the day of the visit, the visiting parent should take the child and observe.

If visiting parents cannot create in their own minds the requisite conversation with their children about what is going on in the children's lives, participating in their lives in this manner will help. Sometimes it helps to bring along your child's friend. The friend can dilute the relationship enough for the other two to relax a little more, and the relaxation may well allow the visiting parent to open up a bit more. Sometimes school projects are group projects, and visiting parents can work with children and their friends in those situations.

In no way am I suggesting that the parent *not* take the child to the show or to the amusement park. What I am suggesting is that those activities ought to be perceived as treats instead of as routine activities which the child automatically (and meaninglessly) learns to associate with the visitation. The child will appreciate the interest and the attention and will come to perceive the visiting parent as loving and caring, even though that parent may not be there very often. The frustration level will decrease in both child and parent. The child will begin to open up more with the parent, and the parent will find that the child will probably initiate much of the conversation, easing the tongue-tied parent's burden. But when there is nothing to say—and frequently, even with good communicators, there is nothing to say—nothing beats a good, sincere hug. That's real quality time.

Perhaps an even more up-to-date cliché might be the "arcade parent" whose role is restricted to providing quarters or tokens so that the child can play the latest electronic games. Perhaps the parent will play too, at least accompanying the child a little more actively in the child's activity. Then the time becomes shared time, at least in part, and that is truly a great gain over the totally detached time spent by the Disneyland parent. Even sharing of activities and experiences to that little degree represented by the arcade parent is better for the child than the withdrawal of the parent who just watches and does little else. The financial pages these days are filled with news about the nationwide collapse of the formerly burgeoning arcade markets. If those storefront parlors disappear, what will the arcade parents do? If they have the motivation to do *something* with their children, they will find something else to do. We have to count on the presence of that motivation or, somehow, try to stimulate it.

In fact, Disneyland parents or arcade parents may be people who really lack the ability to relate verbally or emotionally to their children because of severe personality problems. But if they demonstrate the need to maintain some contact with their children by providing at least passive amusement combined with affection, then that experience is as quality time as the parent can provide. Who should possibly be condemned for doing the best that he or she can do? Sometimes, adult psychiatric patients develop some insight into the fact that the parent whom they grew up hating might not have been able to be anything else, but by then it is usually far too late to attempt renewing the relationship. By then, everybody has lost out.

Most parents, however, have at least some capacity for closeness to their child, and they ought to use it because their children desperately need them to use it. Those parents who can do more with their children but who *don't,* create many problems for their children and probably relieve none. The emotional needs of all children are enormous. The emotional needs of children whose homes have been disrupted because of divorce are even greater—in fact those needs are so enormous that they may be beyond description here, although I shall try hard over the next several chapters. More pertinent, it may be beyond the ability of the visiting parent to recognize these needs. Occasionally, visiting parents may be able to recognize their children's needs but cannot deal with them because of their own problems. Of course, as adults, we realize this can happen, but the tragedy comes because children cannot be expected to understand this.

———— · ————

The following questions are directed to visiting parents, but all parents should try to answer them. No
right or wrong answers are provided here, just the
questions; therefore, search your own experiences,
thoughts, and feelings to determine how you relate
with your kids. (Use this thinking process for the questions provided at the end of each section.)

- Should I take my child to a movie or to another activity I
  hate?

    — Maybe, if the child feels it's *very* important?
    — Even if it's a rock concert?
    — Maybe, if compromise agreements are made with the
      child to do things that I like, too?
    — Sure, because the time shared with the kid is great,
      whatever the activity?
    — All the above? None of the above?
    — More, not listed here?

Divorce and Parents and Kids

Many, if not most, of you who are reading this book are
probably divorced or going through the process of divorcing.
That is a very safe prediction, statistics being what they are. In
1983, the U.S. Census Bureau revealed that the divorce rate
actually went *down* for the first time in more than 25 years.
Much was made of that statistic by fearless optimists, even
though the downward turn was only a minimal, even meaningless, fraction. The divorce rate remains stratospheric. More
than half the marriages which took place in the 1970s and the
1980s will end in divorce. The average length of contemporary
marriages is now a little under 7 years. The number of single-
parent households has jumped astronomically, and these
households are often predisposed to trouble—disturbed rela-

tionships between the children and the single parent living at home, between the children and the visiting parent, between the children and the parent who doesn't visit, or between any and all of them.

This book is not a diatribe against divorce. Thomas Jefferson long ago determined for us that we are entitled to the pursuit of happiness. A loveless existence within any relationship does not fulfill any healthy individual, adult or child. No psychiatrist can say that divorce is a solely evil, unnecessary process. In fact, it can be a very constructive process, not only for the warring spouses but also for the children. They most likely have suffered even more than the adults from the battles or the lovelessness between their parents. Those children deserve to breathe a little easier, without the pressures created within them by the tensions or the predictable fights between their parents.

Family strife before a divorce is dreadful for children, and strife between parents during or following the divorce may harm the children even more. Custody battles, visitation battles, provocative behavior between the separated parents, all increase the child's problems with divorce. Children of divorce deserve to maintain their relationships with both of their parents (and most likely their parents' families as well) even after their parents cease to be husbands and wives to each other. In fact, the children need to *deepen* their relationships with *both* of their parents after the divorce. They need even more security then. Most important, they should not be pawns in the battles between their parents, nor should they serve as objects on which hurt or angry parents vent their guilt, sorrow, or rage.

Practically every parent—married, divorcing, or divorced—will agree with all these principles, at least on the surface. However, things get very sticky and painful in the midst of breaking up a home and a longstanding deep relationship with a man or woman loved so deeply so long. Sometimes even the most well-intentioned people find themselves thinking, feeling, and doing things which violate these principles. Worse, sometimes they do not even recognize what they are thinking, feeling, or doing. If they could step outside of themselves to see objectively, they would probably be horrified and would stop what they were doing. But it is tough to be objective in the eye of a tornado, and that is a pretty good analogy for the turmoil of a marital breakup.

That turmoil is only made worse by the decision on the part of either or both parents to fight over the children. Decisions are made to enter custody battles, to argue over visitation or holiday times, to bad-mouth the other parent before the children, to begin fights when children are returned late or sick, or to do any of the other myriad examples of angry behavior which form significant aspects of the lives of so many children of divorce. Sometimes, when the children are lucky, their parents demonstrate that they can also decide not to do those things.

Divorcing parents must, somehow, find the strength to be open and honest with their children, even if the children are very young.

————— · —————

Nothing succeeds in impressing like honesty. Even young children can sense attempted snow jobs!

————— · —————

Most divorcing parents at least somewhat recognize that they should reassure their children that their problems are with the other parent rather than the children, and that they will continue to love them and to be with them as much as possible even if they are living under different roofs. Verbal reassurances are, of course, urgently important. Their effectiveness, however, is in direct proportion to the parent's determination to keep the promises.

Kids learn soon enough when a parent is a phony, and they can't stand it. They become sullen and morose; then they take out their anger on the parent closer to them. After all, if the children want so badly for the other parent to return and to normalize the household once again—and they nearly always want that—they cannot afford to alienate that parent by venting their anger in that direction. But the custodial parent who demonstrates that he or she always sticks by the kids is the safe one and therefore becomes the recipient of all the expressions of the children's frustration. Fair? Of course not. But divorce always makes it much harder to rear children.

The needs of the children of divorce are the most important factors in planning for their future relationships with both of their parents. By and large in this book, consideration of the wishes or even the needs of adults does not weigh a hell of a lot. Of course, parents have rights, and so do grandparents, adoptive parents, foster parents, and a whole slew of other adults. But those rights count here only when they reflect and second the rights and the needs of the fought-over children of divorce. Those adults who believe that their children are only present to serve their adult purposes, whether or not they are actually aware of believing that, will have a tough time with this book.

———— · ————

The following questions are directed to parents who have custody:

• Have I leveled with my kids about my divorce? And what do I really mean by leveling?

— Have I tried soft-pedaling it? Perhaps to an extreme?
— In contrast, have I indulged myself by telling about all the terrible times I had with their father/mother?
— Have I encouraged them to level with *me* about it?
— If they have, how have I responded? Openly? Defensively?

———— · ————

Longings of the Children

Years of dealing with the tragic adult and child residues of divorce have led me to an inescapable conclusion. A strong campaign must be mounted to alleviate the ill effects of divorce on children. Even though the major thrust of everything said in this book is child-oriented and child-favored, perhaps resulting in an erroneous impression that it is antiparent, I really do wish that even more could be done to mitigate the ill effects of divorce on the parents as well.

Parents are not necessary evils. They are necessary, period, and vastly more often than not they are good, earnest, and worthwhile in their attempts to do the best for their children. Even when the home breaks up, many parents of both sexes continue to press their relationships with their children, working extra hard to maintain those relationships in as unbroken a manner as possible. They do well in their firm determination that their resentments against the opposing spouse will not affect their attitudes toward their children. Sometimes they are able to do that even when they are suffering terribly with their own pain.

Perhaps unfairly, because they are adults, parents are simply expected to follow through. As adults, though, they are also expected to fend for themselves. But divorced, single, or divorcing parents have already developed numerous support groups, and they can always find their own ways to the offices of their friendly local shrinks. The kids do not have that luxury or ability. Besides, they really need their parents, not shrinks.

The basic, universal feeling of all children of divorce is probably best described as an unceasing longing for the parents to reunite so that the home they knew can be reestablished. Research has demonstrated that this longing often persists within the unconscious minds of the children, even into adult life. It can be demonstrated in individuals even after their divorced parents have passed away, long after any realistic chance of parental reconciliation has vanished. That lingering fantasy profoundly affects the types of relationships the children can develop during their own adult lives.

You might find this hard to believe, but the harmful effects of divorce on children are generally deeper and longer lasting than the effects of the deaths of parents. Children may have considerable difficulty understanding parental death, or coping with it, but studies have demonstrated that marital break-ups via divorce can cause far greater emotional reactions in children. The fantasy of parents reuniting is seen only rarely after the death of a parent in an intact family. It is almost always demonstrable in most children following parental divorce.

Parents Who Withdraw

I have already commented on the fact that human children are more dependent for longer periods than the progeny of any other species. Children have obvious security needs which make them totally emotionally and realistically dependent on the stability of the home structure. They count on the familiarity and the relationships they have developed with both parents. Objectively, those parent-child relationships may not have been that productive or constructive, but they were the relationships with which the children became familiar and on which they relied. The loss of those relationships is the major adverse factor affecting the children of divorce. As an example, the ability to count on even the most negatively stereotypical, negligent father *coming home every night,* even to read the paper, to watch television, or otherwise to ignore the child, is a far more positive, stabilizing factor for the child than a visiting parent who ignores the child in other ways such as simply providing passive amusement with no real affection or contact.

Not just visiting parents are at fault here. Parents who maintain custody of their children following divorce may also not provide meaningful contact with their own children. Even if they have fought tooth and nail against their opposing spouses for the custody of the kids, on "winning" them they may simply let them be. We have all seen custodial parents whose time spent with their children is hardly quality time. It is easy to understand why custodial parents sometimes withdraw from children when it is so unbearably difficult to maintain a single-parent household against the enormous odds set up by the economic and other depressing factors of today's real world. What is easy for adults to understand, however, is not necessarily easy for children to understand.

The withdrawn parent is the most common source of hurt or disappointment for a child of divorce. Divorce is a process which can easily lead to withdrawal. Hurt is almost universal in divorce, to the divorcing parents as well as to the children. Parents who lose their spouses and their children are hurt, as well as often angry or vengeful. Withdrawal is a frequent method of dealing with those kinds of feelings which otherwise would be too hard to bear. The parents who win custody are not immune from hurt, either. Their hurt can underlie the lack of quality time spent with their children at home.

The mechanical processes of divorce have become increasingly easy over the years. Many states have adopted no-fault dissolution procedures and community property laws. These allow for divorces to take place without the added agonies of drawn-out courtroom battles and the panic-provoking necessities of charging the opposing spouses with grounds which may have been specifically trumped up for the purpose—and which so often led to countercharges. But no matter how much easier the mechanics of divorce have become, it has not, and most likely never will, become easy for the participants.

However, we must not be sidetracked by sympathy for the suffering divorcing partners; remember that the children are all-important here. As difficult as it is for the parents, the trauma of the family rupture is overwhelming for practically all children. Regardless of their ages, most kids cannot comprehend the basis of the problems between the parents who no longer can get along. The children really should not be expected to understand when most of the parents who are fighting have no grasp of the real reasons either.

———— · ————

The following questions are for visiting parents:

• How have I reassured the kids of my continuing love and support?

— Have I been regular, unfailing in my visits?
— Have I really wanted to be?
— Have I called or written at other times?
— Have I really wanted to? Have I thought about them when I could not be with them?
— Have I spoken seriously with them about not living with them?
— Have I made peace about them with my ex?

Children Who Blame Themselves

Whether they talk about them or not, most children develop strange ideas about the divorces of their parents. Often, they begin to feel that they were at fault. A dreadful, weighty sense of guilt often develops. The children do not discuss that feeling. More often than not, they try to push it out of their minds, but guilt feelings have a way of expressing themselves, often in behavior which is almost guaranteed to provoke punishment. How many divorcing or divorced parents have had to cope with a child whose behavior or attitude is provocative? Child psychiatrists call it "testing behavior," and it is just that. The children test the firmness and the endurance of the parent, hoping underneath that the tested parent will remain firm and will set strong limits against their provocative behavior. The children will then be reassured that they can continue to count on that parent, even in the midst of family trauma. When they become anxious again, as they undoubtedly will, more testing behavior emerges. Most parents find that a sense of humor helps, just as does a good understanding of the testing process.

Frequently, although unwittingly, the guilt feelings may be stimulated or deepened by the attitudes of the parents. Anger toward the other spouse is one very common parental attitude leading to those terrible guilt feelings in the children. So often, panicky and depressed parents "take it out on" the children. Of course, they don't want to. They usually are not even aware that they are doing it, but the children are there and the divorcing spouse is not. Who else, then, is available to bear the brunt of the panicked parent's tension? The result is a feeling within the child that the parent is rejecting him or her. The child begins to feel that the parent somehow blames him or her for the new and upsetting home situation. That feeling of rejection leads to enormous tension within the child who, of course, has no one else to depend on except the parent who is bawling him or her out for totally incomprehensible reasons. Where does the child then go? Where *can* the child then go?

———— · ————

Marriage is a contract representing a willingness, perhaps even more, an eagerness, to invest one's self wholly and completely in a cemented relationship with another person. People get married for a variety of reasons, love and hope representing only two important ones among a large series. They get divorced for a series of reasons at least as long. When, after numerous crises and rebuffs, it is determined that the relationship is not working and can no longer remain cemented, all that frustrated and lost love and hope create a sense of despair and bitterness. The disappointment affecting everyone who loses out in marriage is a terrible burden to bear. No matter how easy the mechanics of breaking the contract become, the hurt and despair last for a long time. Those feelings do not make it easy for parents to visit their children in a home in which they no longer live and in which they no longer feel easily welcomed. But, for the sake of the children, the parent must visit frequently. Those feelings also may not make it easy to rear children when their custody is won, or even during visitation periods. But, of course, children still need to be reared.

All parents and other adult observers will agree that the children of divorce represent the most severely damaged ruins of the process. Most parents will also agree that they should continue to maintain their relationships with the children after the divorce in a manner which at least minimizes that damage. Those of us in the child advocacy business, though, have come to fear that many of those pious promises and agreements may represent no more than lip service to a good and noble cause. Perhaps the parents who do not come through in deed ought not to be condemned because they are, after all, problem-filled and agonized themselves. We understand this. After all, we are sophisticated adults who have been through considerable life experience. But can the children understand this? Should they be expected to?

All the children know is that when the family broke up they were deprived of the protection and dependability provided by the presence of both parents. What this does to them is almost beyond comprehension. No matter how difficult it is to rear children—even in intact families—and no matter how difficult the children themselves may have been to rear, they do not deserve the anxiety and the added burdens created by parents who do not follow through with parental responsibilities following divorce. The children are entitled to far more than lip service. When they do not get it, tragedy can and often does result.

Good parents, married or divorced, provide for their children. Perhaps this book can teach some parents to recognize that they may not actually be doing as much as they could for their children, and that it might actually be better for both the children and for the parents to upgrade their relationships with each other so that quality time really becomes quality time. It is far easier to live when it is unnecessary to kid one's self. It also becomes far easier to rear children.

CHAPTER 2

—— . . . ——

The Ugliest Litigation

For all you divorcing parents planning to get involved in custody battles, the word is, *Don't.* Custody battles are strictly no-win situations. Regardless of who comes out on top in court, both parents and their children lose.

In the mid-1970s, I organized and chaired the first interdisciplinary symposium on problems of child custody suits. In San Diego for that meeting were gathered a select group of 150 participants. To stimulate as much communication among the participants as possible, attendance was restricted to 100 attorneys and 50 psychiatrists, and the parley was addressed by leading psychiatrists, child psychiatrists, and family law attorneys and judges. The proceedings of that conference found their way into the *Bulletin of the American Academy of Psychiatry and the Law* (vol. iv, no. 2 1976, pp. 98-174). At that time, I referred to child custody suits as the ugliest of litigations, and to this date no one has ever argued the point. In fact, *the ugliest litigation* has become a catch-phrase appended by numerous writers and editors to many discussions of child custody suits. They are, indeed, miserable contests, adversely affecting all who participate in them, including the lawyers and judges who must try them.

The Law and Custody Suits

Chapter 1 pointed out that the rights of the contested children of divorce are paramount over the rights of parents and other concerned adults. In many respects, that belief is an extension of the law's official point of view regarding the disposition of the children of divorce. Practically all jurisdictions in the United States and Canada state that the best interests of the children are to be determined to render a constructive decision in contested custody cases. That is how the law is written, but that may not be what courts and individual judges *do*. Different judges may determine differently that the best interests of the children dictate that they be with one or the other parent, depending on the background, feelings, and life experience of those different judges. There is no uniform formula.

Furthermore, the so-called *best interests standard* may not be the only basis used to make decisions regarding the custody of children in dispute. The older *tender years doctrine* may be called into play. According to that theory, children of a "tender age" are automatically perceived as needing to be with their mothers. In contrast, a newer doctrine has emerged, based on the more recent trend of awarding even young children to their fathers. These and other legal bases for custody decisions in contested cases will be discussed in a later chapter. Meanwhile, though, you must remember that all standards may be defined differently and highly individually by highly individual judges. Usually they are defined far differently from the approach of parents fighting for their children.

The late English humorist P. G. Wodehouse commented, "Judges, as a class, display, in the matter of arranging alimony, that reckless generosity which is found only in men who are giving away someone else's cash." Often, warring parents begin to feel that judges adopt the same attitude when they give away other people's children as well! The best way to deal with that— and practically all judges would agree with this—is for divorcing parents to make their own, *mutual* decisions about the disposition of their children and, even more important, *to stick by those decisions.* Like all of us, judges are creatures of their own moods and biases. They may determine that the contested child's best interest is best served by necessarily sending him or her to one parent, a decision generally fought by the other, "losing" parent. The essence of the problem, of course, is not with the judges, or even with the legal system generally. The essence of the problem is that the parents decide to fight over their kids to begin with.

How to Avoid Custody Battles

If parents really want to serve the best interests of their children, they will stop fighting over them. It may surprise parents to learn that they can stop this fighting even while they continue detesting each other for the same reasons which led to the divorce. Parents can and must restrict their fighting to other issues. They can and often do work together to maintain their ongoing parental responsibilities. They may forsake their responsibilities toward each other as spouses, but they must never forsake their responsibilities toward their children.

——— . ———

The best interests of the children are best served when the divorcing parents determine at the outset that they will not enter into any contested custody suit. Furthermore, they must agree that each will maintain continuous, free, and unrestricted relationships with the children, even if one parent is not living in the same household with them.

This means, of course, that each parent agrees that the other parent should have free and easy access to the kids because they recognize that the kids need that easy access to continue those essential relationships. If the parents are able to work along those lines, they will find that they will not only make life a little bit easier for their children (who, nonetheless, will still suffer from the divorce process), but for themselves as well.

Those of us who work in this area already know that nobody benefits from custody suits except the lawyers who command high fees for fighting them. Note, however, that most lawyers detest those battles despite their income-generating potential. That, indeed, is a real testimonial to how miserable those lawsuits are. Even in the midst of considering the high fees such suits generate, most family law specialists grow sick over the effects of the extraordinary stream of vindictiveness they see displayed by the contestants. Many will no longer even accept custody suits as cases, regardless of the fees. More important, many attorneys have become aware that the prizes of the contests, the fought-over children, generally are harmed by the battle instead of benefited. Certainly, most trained, experienced, sensitive judges who specialize in family law recognize that.

Most people who are contemplating going to court over their kids will wonder about these strong opinions and descriptions. If you are among that group, most likely you are already muttering to yourself that I really don't know about *your* situation, about *your* kids, and the terrible damage that bastard, that ex-husband of yours (or, interchangeably, that bitch of an ex-wife) will wreak if he or she gets hold of *your* kids.

Rest assured, I know about those bastards and those bitches. I have seen enough of them in my time. In fact, I have seen enough to maintain and even strengthen my seemingly dogmatic statement that most custody cases harm children regardless of how rotten the opposing spouse may be or is said to be. I know of no experienced mental health experts, be they psychiatrists, psychologists, social workers, or counselors of any type, who hold a different opinion. Most of us with any training in this area have become child advocates, spokespeople for the children of divorce who are the pawns of the battles between their warring parents. We have learned where the real dangers to these kids lie—in the enmity between their parents. Any expression of that enmity by those parents against each other is just like an injection into the children of a dangerous, near-fatal substance.

Most parents do not want to inject their children with a harmful substance. But, in general, they do not recognize that they are harming their children when they enter a custody battle. They rationalize fighting over them because they see benefits to their children from living with them instead of with the hated, opposing ex-spouse. Maybe, in a sense, they are right. Perhaps the parent considering starting a custody battle actually has more to offer the children than the ex-husband or ex-wife. To that I say, "So what?"

My response probably will make little sense to a resentful and hurt parent whose marriage has collapsed. That parent may well see the ex-spouse's wish to seek custody of the children as dangerous. To that parent, the ex-spouse threatens the relationship with the children so carefully established and nurtured over the years of intact home life. Often we hear from those parents that the ex-spouse threatens the very safety of those children. The rub is: most parents who are in the process of going through an exhausting, depressing divorce do not accurately perceive their former mates.

———— · ————

The following questions are directed to parents who have custody:

• What have I told my children about a likely custody battle?

— Have I told them that their lousy father/mother is trying to take them away from me?

— Have I told them that they will probably have to go to court and talk with the judge?
— Have I spoken with them about the concept of visitation regardless of the outcome?
— What have I told myself about a likely custody battle?

Parents Hurt Too

In Chapter 1, I discussed the effects of divorce to some extent, pointing out how the process may have become mechanically easier via community property, no-fault laws, and other shortcuts established by the law to suit our contemporary culture and its standards. But I also warned that divorce has not become emotionally easy and that it probably never will, especially if the divorcing couple entered into their marriage more than casually, with high hopes and a commitment to each other. The loss or failure of that valued relationship leads to personal disaster for each of the divorcing pair, regardless of who files or otherwise stimulates the break.

Hurt, of course, is felt by all parties as part of the personal disaster experienced in divorce. Remember that anger is the almost universal and normal response to being hurt. It is almost inconceivable that a divorcing partner does not harbor at least a modicum of hostility toward the other partner. That hostility assumes many forms and reaches varying degrees, including overt rage at times. It is the principle reason that people misperceive their opposing spouses. Feelings of hurt and anger, conscious or unconscious, cloud the mind and judgment.

Remember, too, that each partner usually sees the other as the cause of the rupture. The unsuspecting spouse who receives divorce papers supposedly out of the clear blue sky probably feels no more disappointment or hurt than the spouse who sees the lawyer first and insists that the papers be prepared.

That spouse, too, must have felt sufficiently disappointed in the relationship, or otherwise hurt by it, to file for the divorce—a very emotionally trying thing to do. You have to think very clearly and objectively about your own divorce to appreciate these observations. Most people going through the process understandably lack that capacity (remember that it is almost impossible to be objective in the eye of a tornado), and they really should not be expected to have it.

If there is a shred of clarity and objectivity present in the thinking of a divorcing partner, my earlier "So what?" may become a little more understandable and sensible. Maybe. "So what?" was my response to one parent's expression that he or she has more to offer the kids than the opposing and resented ex-spouse. But I frankly doubt that most parents involved in custody battles will stop to think about it. The hurt and resentment are still probably too great to allow just about any divorcing parent to step back and see things just a bit differently. In fact, mental health experts who have involved themselves as consultants in custody suits recognize that most battles ostensibly over custody actually represent expressions of the rage felt by the suing parent against the opposing parent. More often than not, the suits have far less to do with the welfare of the children than with the acting out of resentment and hurt.

Nearly every psychiatrist who serves as an evaluator in custody cases has a collection of cases representative of that type of dynamic. I once became involved in a case which eventually became nationally famous because of a renowned television commentator's interest in the controversy. The tempest revolved about three female children, then preadolescent or in their early teens, who had gone to live with their mother following the parental divorce. No dispute was raised about custody at the time of the divorce, but when the mother developed a serious relationship with a male friend, the father became enraged. Most of the father's protests were phrased in terms of his religious standards, which forbade such liaisons. According to the father and his religious supporters, the new openly sexual relationship between the mother and her male friend endangered the moral development of the three girls.

With the aid of his politically astute and very active church, the father mounted a strong campaign in court, and the judge (the father's coreligionist) removed the children from the mother and sent them packing to the father's house. Upon appeal, the state appellate court struck down that decision, noting that no evidence was ever presented to support the father's charges that the relationship with the new male friend harmed the children or that the mother was in any way negligent or inadequate. But the state supreme court subsequently reversed the appellate court, and the battles went on for a number of years. The girls, meanwhile, remained generally unhappy with their father. They saw their mother at prescribed times, and they would stay with her over alternate weekends, but the strength of the antagonistic feelings of both parents began to wear the children down. One became clinically depressed.

In this case, religion provided the rationalization for the rallying cry around which the dissenting parent called his forces. Other cases demonstrate other rationalizations. By examining the situation, however, and even more by examining the dissenting parents, the obvious resentment of one parent toward the other parent becomes transparent. In the case described, the feelings of the father regarding the mother's seeing someone else were nothing short of rageful. Those feelings are very commonly seen. After all, what hurts as much as a wound like that? It is as if the father were saying, "I can barely accept her not wanting me, but when she lets me know that she wants someone else, that hurts too much." Do you know people like that? Do you know the hurt?

———— · ————

What! Me Possessive?

One major issue almost never addressed by battling parents is their possessive attitude toward the children. Earlier, I mentioned that a parent sometimes fights the other parent to prevent the other parent from getting hold of "my kids." The possessive pronoun is urgently important here. The parents themselves may be completely unaware of how strong their sense of possession of the children is. When confronted with evidence of its presence, they may even continue to deny it. Regardless, most act on it.

How much easier the concepts of community property and equitable distribution have made property settlements in this country and in Canada! However, very few battling parents recognize that in a significant sense they conceive of their children as community property. If community property is defined as the collection of items or wealth which has accrued to the couple during the period of time they were together, considered as a product of their working together for it and therefore to be shared, how can the children be seen as anything else? Of course, children must not be perceived as possessions. They are human beings, and the Emancipation Proclamation should have liberated them, too. However, even if the children are inappropriately seen as possessions, it must be recognized that the warring parents may not see them as shared possessions. If the children were seen as community property in the strict sense, obviously that would make life easier because everybody concerned would automatically respond to them by making sure that they were shared equally. There may be too much irony there, but at least that would nip custody battles in the bud.

Even so, this would probably not solve the issue, angry and hurt people being what they are. One problem, of course, is that different people define "equal" differently. As in George Orwell's *Animal Farm*, some animals simply determine that they are created more equal than other animals. The famous story of wise King Solomon illustrates the principle and the problem of attempting to ensure equality. He solved the dilemma of determining the real mother in a contested situation by threatening to slice the baby exactly in two so that each would have exactly half. One of the contestants protested and said that she would allow her rival to take the baby as long as it would not be hurt. Solomon decided that such compassion demonstrated that she was the real mother. Perhaps he was correct. Who can argue with either his reputation or the fact that his approach dealt quickly with the problem and eliminated a long custody battle?

——— · ———

These questions are for all parents to ask themselves:

• How much does the idea that the kids are *mine* affect my thinking?

— How much do I resent him/her doing or buying things for them?
— How much do I resent the children spending *any* time with him/her?
— How often do I think about activities with or plans about the children without considering that their other parent has visitation time?
— What other thoughts or ideas do I have which serve as good examples here? (Be honest, now.)

Joint Custody

A more recent approach to the idea of equal division of the children is found in the burgeoning use of the concept of joint custody. Unfortunately, this rarely works out to be a decision worthy of Solomon if attempts are made to enforce this type of custody disposition against parental resistance in contested cases. Again, the principle is that the parents must share the children equally. Unfortunately, most of the parents who choose this route, and even a number of the judges who make these decisions, do so because they feel that each parent has the right to 50 percent of the children's time and energies.

———— . ————

When joint custody works it is because the parents have correctly determined that *it is the children who are really entitled* to most of both parents' available time and energies.

———— . ————

The parents may not actually share the children equally physically, and one parent may not actually live with them. However, even if one parent lives apart, according to the doctrine, that parent still maintains free and unimpeded access to the children and to their activities. Also, that parent still has the obligation to determine with the parent who lives with the children what the children ought to do in both expected and troublesome situations. Examples include school, health problems, and behavioral difficulties.

When the parents can work together well enough to consult about these matters and to prevent themselves from getting in the way of the children's relationships with the other parents, joint custody represents the best available near-solution to a dismal problem. It tends to smooth over any developing rough spots, and it provides the children with the necessary assurance that each parent respects the other. When it is applied inappropriately, however, it usually creates many more problems than it solves. My own experience echoes the impression of most behavioral scientists that joint custody imposed against resistance usually only provides a legally endowed forum within which chronically angry and vindictive parents can flex their muscles against each other. Their misconception that they are each entitled to an "equal half" lies at the bottom of that.

Children as Property

In contemporary culture, an ambivalence has developed regarding children. In one sense, as has been discussed, it seems as if they are automatically responded to as if they were property. In another sense, the development of ideas about human rights has given us the notion that children, as all people, should be valued for themselves and never as property. Unfortunately, parents are left with mixed and conflicting residues in their minds from both views, and the confusion affects their relationships with their children.

Obviously, if we see them as human beings, children cannot be perceived as inanimate objects which have tangible value and which may be sold or otherwise disposed of in order for each partner to share in the returns for them. Unfortunately, though, the law has seen children in just that light for centuries, and that tradition continues to affect legal judgments made today. Because children had always been seen as property, they were to be awarded (that's still the legal term in use today, so help me!) to the parent who had the better right to property. Until the early years of the twentieth century, from time immemorial, that parent was the father. Of course, divorce was quite rare then, but you might still be surprised to learn that any children of divorce in those days went to their fathers. There were no contested custody suits then. Women had as few rights as children, and certainly lacked the right to sue for custody after divorce.

Usually though, since the turn of the century and until very recently, when thoughts were directed toward the subject of child custody, people automatically assumed that the mother was the usual and preferable source of care for children, especially if the children were very young. You may recall my earlier reference to the tender years doctrine, a legal point of view originally defined in the middle of the nineteenth century but with little influence until the early years of the twentieth century. Then, with the rise of social work and the juvenile justice system, the more humane attitude of seeing small children as other than pieces of property became pronounced. Previously, however, the law had always supported the agrarian or cottage industry background of our society. Children, especially male children, were valued because they were potential workers on the farm or at the loom. Thus, they became especially valuable to the breadwinner, then, as always before, the father. Wives, too, were seen as the property of the husbands who had the legal right (and, as seen then, the moral right) to hold absolute power over their unprotected heads.

Children as property can be seen as a more subtle concept, too. The clearest instances of this are demonstrated by situations in which the children themselves may not really be considered as the real prizes of the competition, even though the battling parent might deny that on the proverbial stack of Bibles. In such cases the parent might value other things even more than the children, although the children provide the wherewithal to gain those other valued things. For example, winning custody of the children might bring material gains. To the victor goes the spoils. In a reasonably well-fixed family, the victor may also get the house—after all, the kids must live somewhere—and the money necessary to maintain it and to rear the children. Perhaps even more important, classically to a divorcing wife and mother, winning may bring some assurance that she will maintain her dependence on her ex-husband. He will necessarily continue to foot many of the bills. Nowadays, with the liberation of women leading to more significant roles for them in the economic marketplace, we may see more and more fathers seeking the same types of dependent states, with the ex-wives providing the bulk of child and spousal support.

The United States has long been described as a child-centered culture. What happens to the fought-over children of divorce makes me believe that it is really a parent-centered culture. The courts generally protect the property rights of parents against the state, against various agencies, or, for that matter, against the children themselves. The concept that children are the property of one or another parent continues to affect the way judges decide who gets the contested children of divorce.

Why in the world does this outmoded and unjust idea continue affecting legal decisions so strongly? Carl Jung, one of the pioneering psychoanalysts, would say that the concept resides in our collective unconscious. Perhaps he was right, but even so, that would be an explanation and not an excuse. All of us at times shake our heads when we are confronted by the seeming reluctance of the law to recognize changes in our society when it instead clings to worn out and even harmful patterns of decision making. Actually, it is appropriate for the law to move slowly, especially if society is moving rapidly. At least some stability is guaranteed that way. Besides, if parents themselves continue to perceive their children as possessions, the law is really only reflecting their views. But it seems that after a hundred years the concept that children are property ought not to continue to represent a foundation of the thinking of many contemporary legislators, court officers, and parents.

———— · ————

The following questions are for all parents who share joint custody of their children:

• How much do I do to ensure that my children's other parent knows as much as possible about the children's lives?

— Do I tell her/him about school, grades, open houses, special projects?
— Do I discuss normal medical matters and medical crises?
— Can I discuss the children's futures with my ex?
— Can we both work to reach some kind of accomodation on an issue we have fought about?
— Do I stimulate the children to contact him/her independently and even to make plans independently?

Who Deserves Whom?

The awarding of contested children to the parents seen as more deserving continues as a major force in U.S. courtrooms. Obviously, a deserving parent may be good for the children, but the very concept of awarding a human child to an overseeing parent is an anachronism. No matter how much the law says that fault is no longer a matter to be determined in a divorce action, divorce procedures and the officers of the courts who oversee them often continue to harbor that concept. That is the origin of the idea that the deserving parent should get the child. In contrast, the nondeserving parent, usually seen as the spouse at fault in the marital disturbance, should not be rewarded by giving him or her that valued property, the child, no matter how much the child might benefit from being placed there.

The celebrated cases of child kidnapping by parents who have been denied custody are sometimes illustrative of this argument. Obviously, the law will not be expected to look with favor on a kidnapper, even if the kidnapper is the child's parent. Keeping in mind the constant instruction that only the child's viewpoint is important here, let us picture a sample case. Suppose that the child is taken at a very early age, and that the child grows up in the care of the kidnapping parent. After several years the other parent succeeds in finding them. What should the courts do then? Should the child be sent to live with the wronged but rightful parent even though that parent is a stranger to the child? Should the child be deprived totally of the only relationship he or she can recall?

Should courts right wrongs done to parents if the children are the vehicles by which the wrongs are righted? Does such a move consider the children's needs? Making awards to the supposedly more deserving parents also seems to violate the concept which supposedly underlies current thinking regarding the disposition of contested children, the best interests standard. That point of view, that the children should go to the parent who can best provide for most of their needs, developed in the mid-twentieth century out of a series of celebrated court cases. Originally pronounced from the bench as case law, it has come to be adopted by numerous state and provincial legislatures so that it has become part of statutory law in most jurisdictions of English-speaking North America.

———— · ————

The *best interests standard* should force the determining judge to ask, "Whom do the *children* deserve?" The idea of determining the more deserving *parent* is not only illogical but is also, really, totally antithetical to the concept of the statute. The parent who seems more deserving on the surface may not actually be the parent who can better fulfill the needs of the disputed children.

———— · ————

I have seen numerous cases in which this surprising turn of events occurred. One especially colorful one which comes to mind revolved about the daughter of a young woman convicted of prostitution a year or so after her divorce. The father sued for custody, claiming that the mother's practices endangered the child. He certainly had an excellent point, although the mother always made sure that the baby was in the hands of competent and consistent caretakers. There was never any contact between baby and pimp. The child was so very attached to the mother that the threat of separation from her led to a severe depression in the child (she had been placed in a foster home during the course of the litigation). The judge, recognizing the trauma represented by the separation, denied the father's petition and kept the custody of the child with the mother. From the bench he also delivered a ringing sermon on the issue that the morality of the mother does not ever *necessarily* adversely affect her relationship with the child. The mother was placed on probation so that the 3-year-old baby could be kept with her.

It would be pleasant and gratifying to report that this story had a happy ending. However, the judge's hope was naive even though his principle was noble. The mother did not curtail her activities, and the father's prediction of endangering the baby was borne out. Tragically, the mother was murdered after a few months by her pimp. The police found her body in her apartment, and they had to tear the clutching, hysterical child away from it.

A more frequently seen situation centers about alcoholism in one of the parents. I recall a case in which the wife's heavy drinking finally led to the husband's filing for divorce. He had tried forcing her into treatment for her drinking numerous times during their marriage, but she had always subverted the attempts. It would appear superficially obvious that the husband ought to have custody of their two preschool-aged children. His own family was handy and could serve as a good back-up. But that was not the way it turned out.

When I examined the woman, it was determined that she had stopped drinking very soon after the husband had moved out. Further, she visited with the children in her in-laws' home frequently, with no ill effects except for tearfulness on everybody's part when it came time for her to leave. Even the in-laws cried! Deeper investigation revealed that the drinking was really her response to the marriage itself, which was not a gratifying relationship for this woman. Although the fact that she resorted to drinking (she had not been a drinker before) did not indicate a strong capacity to deal constructively with stressful situations, her behavior following the separation demonstrated that she was capable of handling the children, who responded more positively to her than to the father. Further interviews with him demonstrated numerous personality problems which would probably have made life difficult for the children just as they had for the wife.

My recommendation, seconded by the judge, was that the children go with the mother, but that she must seek and continue psychiatric treatment which could strengthen her. For the record, it should be pointed out that she is doing well now. After a couple of years, she was able to see her therapist less and less. She also made excellent progress in the job she found the nerve to take only with the backing of her treatment. She eventually remarried, and the children, now adolescents, are happy and healthy. Their father, unfortunately, has seen them less and less, although his parents continue their doting relationship with them as fond grandparents.

———— · ————

The following questions are directed to the hopefully few parents who have custody and whose children have been taken by the parent without legal custody:

- Honestly, now, searching back—what did I do that might have stimulated my ex to steal *my* kid?

  — Have I prevented visitation or been otherwise provocative?
  — Have I continued to fight over just about everything?
  — Have I failed to pick up signals, cues, or clues he/she might have given?
  — Have I failed to alert school or nursery to stick with the prearranged schedule, or failed to notify them of a change in the schedule?
  — Any or all of these, or more? (Honestly, now.)

Kids and Judges

Regardless of the best interests standard and what it ought to mean, many judges continue to function as if the fault concept in divorce were still the law of the land. No-fault divorce is the law now in 48 of the 50 states and through much of Canada. Recently, in Illinois, a new law allows for the optional use of no-fault divorce, although the old fault system is still retained there as an alternative. With no-fault divorce, neither party in a divorce action can be considered at fault in the breaking up of the relationship: There is no bad guy. The marriage simply is considered no longer viable. Regardless of what the law *says,* some judges insist on perceiving one or the other spouse as a bad guy.

Through the centuries, judges have been in the business of making awards to wronged people, to wronged states, or to wronged populations. After all, the children do not bring the suits, the adults do. In child custody suits, the law describes one parent officially as the plaintiff and the other as the respondent. Therefore, one must be wrong and the other right, if a legalistic frame of reference is used. Unfortunately, many judges are not specifically family law judges. They may not be trained in those areas of concern which should be at the fingertips of those people who have to make decisions about children. Their legal backgrounds unfortunately force them to think legalistically if they have not become sensitized to the human development issues which ought to underlie the decisions.

This is no slap at judges. They are supposed to be experts in the law, not in child development. Even experienced, perceptive, and sensitive family law judges, who may have taken special training in this area, recognize that they often need help from experts regarding the best interests of disputed children. But legalistic thinking continues to rear its head in courts. After all, it is *supposed* to rear its head there. That is one very major reason why courtroom decisions about the disposition of fought-over children are often so harmful to all concerned. Legalistic thinking may not be in the children's best interests.

——— · ———

Legalistic thinking always leads to one litigant winning and the other losing. The children always lose because they have been dragged through the mill in the first place.

——— · ———

Time spent in court, or anxiously waiting for it to be over, is surely not quality time! Usually the children lose for other reasons as well, including the compounded hurts suffered by both parents in the conflict. Gravely wounded parents often react to the traumatic decisions of custody battles by withdrawing from their families even more than the divorce process might cause them to. The ex-husband of the alcoholic mother I described before is a good example. In some cases, the winning parent might appreciate the losing parent's withdrawal. Perhaps he or she might even be relieved and gratified by it, but it is harmful to the children who need to continue an unbroken relationship with the withdrawn parent.

———— · ————

Declaring one parent right and the other parent wrong is harmful to the children.

———— · ————

After all, they are the offspring of the so-called wrong or bad parent as much as they are of the so-called right or good parent. What effect does this name-calling have on the minds of young children who are just beginning to develop self-images? Children are always told that they are just like one parent or the other. If the parent they are told they resemble suddenly becomes a so-called bad parent, what does the child then begin to think about himself or herself? Parents who stimulate custody battles are *both* wrong because they create self-doubt in their children.

Remember my response to the parent who says that he or she has more to offer the children than the other parent does. To refresh your memory, I said, "So what?" Remember also that only the child's definitions of what is important count here. With these warnings in mind, we must conclude that both parents together have the most to offer the children—and the children need the most. That obviously does not mean that the parents must continue living with each other despite their inability to do so or their wish to separate. What it does mean is that their separation must not lead to their children being permanently deprived of either of them.

The legalistic approach which "awards" the contested children to one parent, even to possibly the better parent, always creates hurt for the children. No matter how much one parent has to offer, that parent can never compensate the children for the loss of the ongoing, free relationship with the other parent. Even if the actual relationship with the other parent was not seen as free or rewarding by outside observers, it was valued by the children.

You may be surprised to learn that many children even continue to value relationships with poor, even abusive parents. They do not ordinarily value the abuse, but they value the hope or the fantasy that the abusive parent will cease his or her abusive behavior and will love them as they always wanted to be loved. The loss of that ongoing contact with that parent may dash those hopes for reconciliation and fulfillment.

In one sense, of course, that may not be very damaging. After all, in reality the loss of a parent who is deficient may not be comparable to the loss of an adequate, loving parent. Nonetheless, if often leads to a continuing sense within the child that he or she lacks the capacity to "make it" with that parent. The child will often think of himself or herself as defective in such instances, and will be crippled to some extent in being able to "make it" in other relationships as well.

———— · ————

These questions are for those parents who have lost custody:

• How did you respond to losing a custody battle?

— Did you withdraw? How did that affect the kids?
— Did you resume the legal battle? How does *that* affect the kids?

— Did you complain to the children during your visits
with them which you perceive as too restricted?
— Have you let your anger at your ex-spouse be misdi-
rected at your children?
— Have you become depressed? If so, what have you
done about that?

When Parents Fight

Earlier I pointed out that the greatest dangers to children
of divorce lie in the expressions of continued enmity between
their parents. Battles, even physical battles between still-mar-
ried parents, generally create less long-term anxiety within the
children than do the hostilities expressed in custody battles.
While the home remains intact, the children usually think in
terms of the family staying together despite the quarreling.
Even that fantasy provides at least some temporary relief. After
the parents actually break up and the home is shattered, further quarreling between them only deepens the wounds of the
breakup, which may already be too much for the children to
bear. If the children are staying with one parent, even uneasily,
the idea of shifting or changing is terribly frightening to them.
They recognize and dread the instability inherent in such a
move. Think also about the feelings of the parent who must
part with the children and about what those feelings do to the
children.

The rage of either parent cannot help but spill over to the
children. It is almost inconceivable that they can possibly be
shielded from it. Certainly when any counselor speaks with any
parent in a contested custody case, the parent nearly always
spouts pious comments about *never* letting the children know
just how much he or she detests the opposing spouse. Not only
that, the parent will usually discuss his or her knowledge that
the children are *never* to become involved in interparental hostility and that the parents know how necessary it is for the

children to maintain good relationships with and high opinions of both parents.

Sure they do. They really do. At least they think they do. However, in their own overwhelming hurt and resentment, they cannot be expected to act on what they know at all times. Remember the eye of the tornado, that analogy for the divorce action. Divorcing parents are prisoners of emotions which may well carry them away from reason and prevent them from recognizing what they are actually doing to their children. Counselors often must work hard to maintain their own recognition of this. Unfortunately, many become angry at parents who involve children in custody suits. They see those parents as self-serving and as harmful to their children. The anger of counselors does not cause parents to recognize what they are doing to themselves or to their children. I know my own anger never helped any of my own patients!

Fortunately, in a large sense the lives of children do not completely revolve about their parents. Much in their lives is outside of the home. Friendships, school, and other activities take up considerable time and energy and make up a great part of the child's world. However, threatening the stability of that world by threatening to take the child away *when the parents are no longer together* (unlike in, for example, a *family* move across town or even across the country) leads to clinically demonstrable symptoms of anxiety and depression in many of these children.

Many adults tend to shrug off the possibility of long-lasting emotional disturbances in children. Because children maintain their capacity for growth and development, many adults consider that kids can "bounce" easily and can recover quickly from passing hurts or other problems. Or, if they don't "bounce," then, according to those adults, the children will probably outgrow their troublesome situations or responses. As a practicing psychiatrist, I can state definitely that, were such statements to be true, neither I nor any of my colleagues in the mental health professions would ever have patients to see. But patients are plentiful because children do not bounce into good mental health or outgrow their anxieties. Their troubles simply go underground to emerge later in life.

———— • ————

These questions are directed to all parents:

- How much do you *really* guard against bad-mouthing the other parent?

  — In front of the kids?
  — In front of anyone else as well?

- How much secret satisfaction do you *really* feel when the children may bad-mouth him/her, too? (Level with yourself here.)

What the Children Need

We are all as we grow up to be, and our growing up is colored and altered by our experiences. A very significant portion of those experiences is affected by the relationships between us as children, and our parents. Children learn to perceive the world around them via the perception of their own, personal world. At first, that world is the immediate family. The perceptions of the immediate family remain as the nucleus of the widening world for the growing infant and child, and then the child's world gradually enlarges to take in the other institutions affecting it. Each successive, wider concentric circle is affected by the experiences in the preceding, smaller one. The experiences with the parents remain the most basic and fundamental, and they color all subsequent significant relationships in our lives.

In addition to the self-image problems created by children's being prevented from relating freely to one parent, children need free and open access to both parents for many other reasons. First of all, the children begin to perceive the parent whom they are not allowed to see freely as rejecting, just as much as they would a physically abusive one. If the parents separate, the children need to know that they can continue to see and relate to the noncustodial parent almost as freely and as easily as they had before, when the parent used to come home or stay home regularly. Of course, they know that they cannot actually do that because of the physical circumstances of the living situation, and they will be very threatened by that knowledge. Therefore, it is essential that the custodial parent continue to reassure and to demonstrate to the children that such unlimited and unrestricted access is not only possible but preferable. Obviously, it is also essential that both parents communicate with each other about the children. Rancor about everything else must be set aside when the topic is the children.

Of course, absent parents are part and parcel of the inner, emotional lives of children even when they are no longer around. However, those inner memories, hopes, feelings, and longings often fester and plant the seeds for later problems if the actual relationship with that parent does not proceed and develop into some kind of maturity. No matter how old at the time of the marital rupture, the children were molding their identities and their very existences around the structure provided by the presence of both parents. Being unable to count on the presence of the noncustodial parent if ever and when ever that parent may be needed cannot be compensated for by even the most willing, skilled, or wealthy single parent. The most skilled single parent makes sure that the children maintain a healthy and an open relationship with the parent who is not at home—if that parent will allow it and if that parent does not withdraw. The noncustodial parent might withdraw anyway, but the odds that he or she will withdraw are much greater if there had been a custody battle. Kids do not deserve that kind of outcome from a divorce.

I am asking a great deal here from both parents, but not as

much as the children ask. Never mind that the absent parent may have already established a liaison with a new and resented potential mate; never mind that the custodial parent may have done the same thing; never mind that the problems leading to the original divorce continue to simmer: The children are in need, and both parents must work very hard to fulfill those needs. However, just try to picture that attempt following a drastic and bloody custody battle between those same parents!

Always remember, human children are born the most helpless of all species, and they remain helpless relatively longer. They need to depend upon their parents; if they cannot, anxiety is the universal response. This is why divorce itself is so difficult for children. When the problems of divorce are amplified and compounded by the problems of a custody battle, the children really suffer in spades.

Nothing is left for children to count on during a custody battle. After a divorce, a wise parent can work reasonably successfully at reassuring children that their home will remain their home and that their relationships with both parents will remain sacrosanct. Such reassurances will go far to relieve some of the anxiety generated by the parental breakup. However, if the divorcing parents decide to fight for the kids, no such reassurances can be given. Even if one parent decides to provide phony reassurance, the children know that it is phony. The other parent will tell them, or a neighbor, or the neighbor's children. The children simply cannot be shielded.

———— · ————

The following questions are directed to parents who have custody:

• How do you help the children handle their feelings about a parent who withdraws or otherwise fails on a number of occasions to follow through?

— If the children are old enough, do you discuss this with them?

— In your opinion, how old should the children be to discuss this openly?
— In your discussions, are you nonjudgmental?
— Do you go so far as to accuse the negligent parent?
— Do you derive secret satisfaction from the children's disappointment?

Putting the Kids in the Middle

Sometimes adults feel that a custody battle may actually provide reassurance for the children that they are loved. For that matter, so does abdominal surgery, if the children need operations and the parents provide them! These battles are really set up to demonstrate to the battling adults they they love the children more than the opposing spouses do. Since the motivations for many custody suits generally have little to do with love for the children, an adult still selling a phony posture to a child sows the seeds of destruction in a relationship sorely needed by that child. Certainly, children can be seduced into buying this bit of self-promoting, if often false, information which says, "I love you more." But the price the children pay for it is too high. The price is at least tentative belief in negative information about the other spouse, who, by the way, also happens to be a parent to those children. How should children feel if they receive negative opinions from one parent about the other parent?

One parent's bad-mouthing of the other must adversely affect the children, who then begin suffering because of divided loyalties. Children ask themselves, "How can I continue to love Mommy/Daddy if I continue to love Daddy/Mommy?" Inevitably, loyalty conflicts are part and parcel of custody battles, and they tear children apart emotionally. Sometimes those conflicts are worsened by well-meaning but grossly misinformed judges or others who ask the children their preferences in these battles.

As a general rule, mental health professionals maintain the opinion that children are not to be asked their preferences because asking them always puts them on the spot. No matter which way they answer, they lose. At least, they expect that they will lose the love and affection of the parent whom they did not choose. Often, their expectation is borne out. The hurt to a parent who is told that his or her child prefers to live with the other parent must be terrible. Such hurt cannot help but affect the parent-child relationship.

Most often, of course, children will not answer a preference question directly. Pressuring does not help the situation. They will usually persist in their response that they want their parents to live together again. The children should be allowed that response; after all, it is true. Being made to express a preference for one parent over the other will only create enormous guilt feelings in the children. The harbored feelings of guilt will lead to depressions and other symptoms of emotional disturbance in later years. Before then, though, being made to express a preference will harm the relationships with *both* parents. Obviously, the feelings of guilt over rejecting one parent will affect the relationship with the rejected parent. What is generally not recognized, though, is that the supposedly preferred parent may well become the focus for the child's considerable hostility later on, based on resentment over having to sacrifice the other parent.

Even the law recognizes these problems about child preference to some degree. Most courts will not accept the preferences of very young children, although there remain some judges who will either take these kids into their chambers and ask them privately, or, worse yet, ask them in open court. By statute, most jurisdictions will listen to children above the age of 14, and more often than not the courts will go along with those preferences unless there are cogent reasons not to do so. The law's obvious rationalization is that adolescent children are more capable of exercising the requisite judgment to make these decisions. Of course, for the most part that is a fallacy.

Even parents in intact families will attest to the enormous defects characteristic of adolescent judgment, especially in emotionally loaded situations. So often, parents must try to undo some of the problems resulting from those defects in adolescent judgment. Adolescents can be torn apart and bribed just as easily as younger children, and they do not "bounce" any easier.

Sometimes, during their investigations of the parties in custody battles, psychiatrists hear the preferences of children. The task for a psychiatrist in such a situation is to understand the meaning of what the child is saying. Why does the child say what he or she says? What is the real message the child is attempting to express regarding her or his relationship with each parent? The preference itself may be meaningless, but the need for the child to express it may be very important.

Often, children may be overtly or covertly encouraged by a parent to state a preference. The children may actually be coached. I recall one case in which I interviewed two small girls who were being fought over. Their grandparents were actually rearing this pair of sisters. Their mother had moved out, and the father then took the girls with him back to his parents' home. As might be expected, considerable bitterness was expressed by all the adults in that household toward the mother, although the girls maintained regular and happy visits with her. Following a pleasant session with the girls, I was preparing to dismiss them when the older one, then 9 years old, began a transparently memorized speech about her mother having broken God's commandments because she had committed adultery. It was delivered rapidly and without any of the spontaneity or feeling characteristic of her previous expressions with me. The older girl stumbled over some of the words she had been taught to say. I had to help her with some, but not with either "commandments" or "adultery." She knew those well. When I thought she was finished, I commented to her that she must have felt a real need to tell me all that in the way she did. However, I was mistaken; she had not finished. Instead, without any apparent notice of my comment, she went on with more of the rote memorandum!

Obviously, I learned a lot more about the relationship between the girls and their father and his parents by virtue of that coaching than I did about the girls' real feelings toward their mother. Like so many girls in that same situation, these two were being harmed by the vituperative comments about their mother. After all, she is the person with whom they had formerly been closest and with whom they were very appropriately beginning to identify. The problems which will affect their developing self-images, based on identification with a person whom they were being taught to hate, will emerge later in the form of self-hatred, a most unenviable and troublesome trait.

Not only the rage between the parents poses problems for the children of divorce. When custody battles are fought, the parents become tremendously anxious. If you have ever gone to court, you will understand this to some degree. Litigation, with its constant badgering in the form of examinations, interrogatories, declarations, depositions, preliminary or other *pro forma* hearings, and, then, finally, a trial, with direct and cross-examination before a judge always perceived as a frightening figure, scare the hell out of most of us. When the stakes are as meaningful as one's children, the process and outcome are faced with even more tension and dread.

Anxiety is even more catching than the measles. Who needs anxious parents? Certainly, the children of divorce, already suffering from the breakup of their homes, don't need that complication. But again they cannot be shielded because the parents will not be shielded from the anxiety-provoking aspects of the battle. Rearing children after a marital breakup is a difficult task when there are no complications. A custody suit is a real complication! The anxiety within the parent who has custody until the trial creates even greater anxiety in the children. School problems, health problems, behavioral problems, and interpersonal difficulties with other kids are frequently seen. A good parent will, of course, attempt to assuage the anxiety of the children. Can a parent who is being made increasingly anxious do that?

Please, please, consider very carefully the effects of a custody battle. There is no quality time there for anybody.

———— · ————

The following questions are directed to parents who are battling for custody:

- How much do you encourage your children to verbalize wishes for you as the preferred parent?
- How much do you do this in ways you are unaware of? (Think hard and be very honest with yourself. No one else is listening.)

CHAPTER 3

· · ·

Uglier Yet

I have a vague and nagging fear that some of you may not be hearing me. You must understand how important it is to avoid custody suits and fighting over your children during and after divorce.

Do you think my warnings in the previous chapter were too subtle? Maybe they were too low-key, preventing you from getting the drift. But if you have stuck with me for this long, I can hope that a little more information about the harmful effects of custody battles will eliminate them completely from your mind. That will be a great step toward ensuring quality time for your children and for you.

Lawyers and Custody Suits

Custody battles cost a lot of money. Divorces themselves cost a lot of money, for the most part, and whenever there are fought-over issues (despite the often-healing influences of community property, there are still frequent issues to fight about when people want to fight) the costs escalate. Lawyers charge high fees, and good lawyers often charge even higher fees. Courtroom battles skyrocket the ante.

The money spent on battling is obviously better put to use by the divorcing parents who will still need to support their kids as well as themselves. Separate households add expenses to each participant not even dreamed of when the battle is joined, and the disentangling partners are often caught short by that recognition. The rather bitter joke about being unable to afford a divorce is told often. Sometimes it is true, but, again, the emotional costs to all concerned of staying in a loveless, unrewarding, and, in the end, hurtful marriage are probably even higher than the financial costs of divorce.

When a custody battle is decided by one or both litigants in a divorce action, the lawyers should let their clients know just what might happen. Custody battles bring forth out of the sewers all the ugly aspects formerly accepted as a standard in divorce trials that have, fortunately, not been part of routine divorce actions since the era of no-fault. Some of us are old enough to recall the more sensational, very juicy divorce trials of years ago, when the reputations of each party were dragged through more than mud. Private detectives trailing each partner to dig up unsavory items, tales told out of school (or out of the bedroom)—all whetted the public's appetite for scandal. Now, with divorce so much easier mechanically, only custody trials serve to provide the same treats to the public. The old Roman emperors kept their weary and downtrodden people happy by providing them with bread and circuses. Now newspaper details of custody battles may do the same thing.

I have commented on the retention of the fault doctrine in the minds of many judges who decide custody suits—judges may tend to direct children to the more deserving—that is, less faulty—parent. Lawyers know that, and many prepare their cases by besmirching the character of the opposing spouse. Especially when a father is attempting to gain custody, the father's lawyer may attempt to paint the mother as unfit on any grounds she or he can either dig up or invent. Lawyers know that fathers still have an uphill battle, especially when they try to gain custody of small children, although the battle is certainly not as uphill as it used to be. In fact, a number of judges, in their attempts to be "with it," often go out of their way to award children to fathers. But, for the most part, the odds still favor mothers in these actions, unless the father and his attorney can demonstrate that she is unfit. It gets ugly.

The ugliness might be dismissed by stating that the adults ask for it and that they enter the custody arena with their eyes wide open. My impression is that they really lack true appreciation of the ugliness before they are inundated in it, even if their lawyers try hard to teach them about it. But, in any case, the children do not ask for the ugliness. They do not know what is in store for them. They respond to the anxieties of their parents, and also to the allegations tossed back and forth between the hostile parties. They are torn by those countercharges. Loyalties are tested, and why in the world should a child's loyalty to a parent ever be tested? The actual identities of children are tested. Children who have always been told that they are just like one of their parents now begin to wonder if that's so good—after all, look at how the parents are being painted.

Many of my colleagues dislike divorce lawyers intensely because they feel that they lack compassion for the suffering children of divorce. My own experiences with lawyers are not quite as damning. I pointed out earlier that many lawyers will not even try custody battles because of their own considerable compassion for the children. After a period of time on a family court bench, many judges have to transfer to a less stressful trial calendar. Believe it or not, many find criminal cases easier. All they deal with there are such simple issues as rape and murder.

But, sorry to say, just as some mental health professionals glory in these courtroom antics and charge as much as possible for their testimony, some attorneys work hard at fighting as dirty as possible, regardless of the effects on the children involved. In fact, a recent book by a very successful and colorful divorce attorney has received considerable publicity. The book happens to be directed at the large number of hurt and disappointed men who feel that they have been disenfranchised by the divorce system, and it is written to appeal to their crassest motives.

In the book, as well as in interviews about the book, the attorney milks the idea that child support and associated extra payments to the divorced spouse are wasted expenditures. He suggests fighting for the children to save money in the long run. The book has nothing in it representative of any sensitivity to the effects of the battle on the children or even to the idea that the mother might have been the more appropriate single parent for those children. By and large, he decries the idea of the best interests standard. I suppose that lawyer-authors will also write books appealing to disenfranchised mothers who feel cheated out of having their children. Will those books also center about financial motives, and will they also stimulate further courtroom battles which hurt the children so very much?

———— · ————

These questions are directed to parents who are battling for custody:

• Secretly, do you really miss the old days of always-nasty divorce?
• Do you really look forward to dragging your ex through the mud?
• Do you need to do that so badly that the needs of the children take second place?
• Do you want the children to think and feel the same about your ex as you do?
• Is that an underlying reason for entering this battle? (Honestly, now.)

Who Depends on Whom?

Some of you object to my overall damnation of custody battles when, as you probably see it, letting your children live with your ex would be disastrous. Of course, the questions must always be asked, "Disastrous to whom?" "Why should it be?" The experts who evaluate the battling parents and children in custody suits must ask themselves these questions. They must always attempt to understand the real underlying motives of the combatants. Those, too, may represent dirty linen hung out in the courtroom. Sometimes, they find that the motives are wholesome and realistic and that the parents each feel that their having the children is actually best for the children. But, more often than not, the motives for battle are nowhere near as pure.

Money has already been described as the basis for many custody battles. That represents a major, if superficial, motivation. Psychiatrists and psychologists who interview parents in these wars often find that many factors operate beneath the surface. The parents themselves may not be at all aware of some of the more devious reasons causing them to start the suits. Just as a single example, a frequently seen reason that parents start suits is their dependency on their child, when one would think that the dependency ought to be the other way around.

Who has a greater need for the other, the child or the parent? Don't jump to the conclusion that the children need the parent more than the parent needs the children. If you do, you'll be wrong, at least in some cases. The parents don't need the children more in most cases, fortunately, but the situation is not that uncommon. When it does occur, it creates a great deal of trouble for both the parents and the children. When it is uncovered and discussed by the examining mental health professional, embarrassment may be the least of the results.

An enormous amount of self-examination in a climate of complete and open honesty is required before a parent recognizes that it is actually he or she who has the need which sets the battle into motion. If you are now in the eye of a tornado, pause for a moment and take a deep breath so that a little time for self-evaluation and a bit of honesty can have some effect. Let me tell you a little bit about the dynamic of parents depending on children. To appreciate it more, look at the associated idea of the need for some parents to stay together instead of, more appropriately, divorcing. Often, parents unknowingly manifest many dependent needs.

The existence of a parent's need for her or his children certainly does not mean that the children do not need that parent. Of course they do, and the other one as well, and, as a matter of fact, all the family and extended family support and love they can possibly collect about themselves. They need it even more following a parental breakup than before, because when they have a family sufficiently intact to maintain a superficial structure, they may not feel the same sense of abandonment or of drifting that they do after the separation.

But, as I commented before, children do not institute lawsuits for custody. If they could, the odds would probably favor their attempting to force a legally imposed reconciliation between their parents. Most likely they would try to force that reconciliation, even if they recall only too painfully the dreadful battles which led to the divorce and which frightened them so terribly before one or the other parent finally moved out.

———— . ————

The following questions are directed to parents who are battling for custody:

- If you continue to insist on fighting over the kids, what do you think will happen to you if you lose?

  — Are you prepared for that possibility?
  — If you feel that losing would be a crushing blow, are you prepared to recognize that you may have needed

the children as much as you thought they needed you?
— How will you deal with your sense of loss?
— Will you withdraw or continue your relationship with them?
— Will you foist your hurt and anger on them?

Staying Together for the Kids: Another Fallacy

All the comments about the needs of children for intact families should not cause any divorcing parent to consider reconciliation for the sake of the children. Reconciliation must be weighed exclusively on the basis of the odds for reaching and maintaining a mutually rewarding marital relationship. Without such mutuality, the resulting friction and frustration would only lead to problems in the children anyway. Perhaps those problems would be even greater than those stimulated by the divorce, although it is doubted that they would be as great as those stimulated by a custody battle.

When parents think at all about the effects of their marital strife on their children, they usually perceive the children as generally very unhappy and anxious. Those are about the limits of recognition in the eye of the tornado. Parents rarely consider the effect of the battle on role modeling. Children must be taught about marriage. They need to know what it should be and what it actually is. What it actually is ought to be what it should be, but we know from experience that there may be a real gap between those two levels. If they are to learn about adult relationships (as differentiated from relationships which may occur between adults), children must learn to identify with adults who are able to give and take in a good and stable marriage relationship. When adults cannot do that, marriages suffer, and they often break up.

Role models break up then, too. Marital harmony leads to the development for children of role models which allow them to perceive marriage in a positive and hopeful light. The adult capacity to quarrel and then to resolve the conflicts is a valuable trait. It can be learned by children who see their own parents as able to do that.

However, marital disharmony leads to continued open conflict or to other manifestations of mutual aggression. Sometimes that mutual aggression may not be as open or as overt as in out-and-out fighting, but even so, children have little opportunity to observe the process of conflict resolution. Continuing a marriage which consists mainly of interparental battles provides no favor for the children. They learn all the bad things, and their futures as marital partners are placed in jeopardy.

Remember that the battles need not be forceful or even overt for the children to be affected. For example, one parent may take an active, overtly dominant role while the other is apparently subordinate. However, the apparently subordinate parent may not be subordinate under the surface. Perhaps that parent gives out subtle, demeaning messages (usually complaints) about the other parent. The recipients of those messages are the children, who will then begin to become confused about their relationships with the other parent and about their feelings toward him or her. What kind of role model does the manipulating parent provide? What kind of collective role model does a pair of battling parents provide? What do children learn about solving problems in such a situation? What do they learn about starting problems?

In Marin County, north of San Francisco, Dr. Judith Wallerstein and her associates have made an ongoing study of the children of divorce. It should come as no surprise that they have concluded that the process of breaking up the family is usually very stressful to the children who have been observed and evaluated for over 10 years. They determined that many of the children responded to their family breakups with rage and depression and often with great fear that they would have no one to turn to for dependable support.*

Many of the articles and books which have resulted from the Wallerstein group's research quote numerous comments by the children they interviewed. Many of these quotations indicate that the children would have preferred their families to remain intact despite the problems. A number of other observers, after reading these articles with these very moving expressions of the children's feelings, have begun to resurrect a notion we had long thought to be outmoded—that it is always best to keep the disturbed families together, regardless of the problems, solely for the sake of the children. Many have written articles and even books in which that idea is accented. However, most behavioral scientists, including Dr. Wallerstein, disagree. In fact, her latest data indicate that even the children of divorce, after 10 years, have begun to recognize that the divorces of their parents were probably necessary and even constructive.

Certainly, we must accept the often-demonstrated fact that the problems of the children of divorce were frequently stimulated by the original problems between the parents. The frequent quarrels between the parents who had not yet split provided the framework for many personality difficulties and other emotional symptoms in their children. Just as certainly, we must also accept the equally valid fact that many problems of the children of divorce are stimulated by the divorce itself. However, even if we accept both of those very true statements, we must remember that *the problems of the children of divorce are significantly worsened by the destructive behavior of the parents during and after the divorce.* Those problems may be set into motion by the parental quarrels leading to the divorce, and they may be stimulated further by the divorce process itself, but it is the behavior of the parents toward the children *following* the

---

* Wallerstein, J. S., & Kelly, J. B., *Surviving the Breakup: How Children and Parents Cope with Divorce*, NY, Basic Books, 1980.

breakup which is crucial in determining the nature and extent of the children's problems. In the majority of instances, this factor and its effects are what Wallerstein and her group were describing.

———— · ————

The extended withdrawal of one parent following the divorce hurts the children terribly. So does the prolonged preoccupation of the custodial parent with the struggles of single life, including single parenthood. Any of the other problem sequels to the divorce itself, if continued for long times, present drastic threats to the children. But, of all these, the manipulative expression of rage toward the opposing spouse by one or both parents hurts the children the most.

———— · ————

Living together for the sake of the children when there are so many problems between spouses undoubtedly creates enormous problems for the children. Just as a single example, the resentment each frustrated and stuck parent must begin to feel toward the children has to affect them. Inevitably, the children are unconsciously and unwillingly perceived by the parents as the ropes that bind them together in a loveless and hated relationship. Ministers, psychiatrists, and counselors of all types have observed those feelings for years. When it comes time to treat the children of those bound and enforced marriages in psychotherapy, the effects are heard loudly and clearly.

Unlike the abuse of quality time, parents definitely are not rationalizing when they conclude that their living together may be more destructive to the children than their breaking apart. In fact, experience often shows that couples who can reach that decision may well be more likely to work harder at maintaining their own relationships with their children after divorce than those couples who do not consider the effects of their continuing but destructive marriages on their children. Perhaps the couples who can and do consider this may be those for whom counselling might provide answers to the problems, thereby leading to a more successful marriage, a more successful divorce, or to a more successful subsequent marriage. In any case, it is apparent that these are thinking and considering couples, and thinking and considering parents, in or out of marriage, are what the children need. Self-congratulatory, sacrificing, or even martyrizing couples who stay with each other for the sake of the children are not what they need.

———— · ————

The following questions are for all parents:

• What do you teach your children about love and marriage (not sex, but love and marriage)?

    — Do you talk with them about your own failures?
    — Do you discuss successful marriages?
    — Do you know some?
    — Do you expose the children to them?
    — Do your negative, sour attitudes speak louder than your positive words?

Dependent Parents

Haven't we all recognized that the idea of staying together just for the sake of the children can be an even more blatant rationalization than "quality time?" Let's return to the question posed earlier about parental dependency on children: Just whose needs are being met in custody suits, anyway?

Children are not the only creatures in this world who have dependent needs. Adults are sometimes just as prone, although they may not perceive their own needs as clearly as they perceive their children's. Of course, children are permitted to have needs. Adults, they often tell themselves, are not. In a sense, of course, they are right, but very few people grow up without dragging with them residues of their childhood frustrations. Nearly all of us manifest some infantile or childhood impulses which occasionally get in the way of possibly fulfilling adult relationships. Who among us is "adult" all the time, with the requisite degree of perfect tolerance and humor and with a total lack of selfish feelings which must be gratified instantly?

Often, when people grow up deprived of relationships with their own parents that provide the security and identification strengths they needed, they remain stuck in the same childhood longing patterns described in the children of divorce. In childhood and adolescence, growth into a subsequent stage of psychosocial development proceeds only after the preceding stage has resulted in some kind of satisfaction. If only frustration and conflict resulted during that earlier stage of growth, no building blocks will have been formed for the necessary next steps. Thus, telltale infantile patterns leave their marks on the individual's feelings, responses, and behavior.

As a very frequently seen example, unfulfilled dependency needs from childhood often cause adults to stick with a marital partner who provides little if any satisfaction or gratification. Doing so may, in one sense, relieve anxiety, because those spouses who stay feel assured that they will be taken care of. However, the emotional price they pay for the fulfillment of these infantile needs is usually enormous. The frustration felt in that situation often spills over into the relationship with their children, who are then seen, of course, as rivals for the other parent. The children need the other parent, as does the dependent parent. An actual sibling rivalry situation therefore results between the dependent parents and their children, a situation not at all likely to be rewarding for either parents or children.

One of the most significant issues manifest in this situation is a generation-to-generation trail of dependent parents who do considerable harm to their own children. They make their children into adults who, like their parents, remain childlike and dependent throughout their own adult lives. Their childlike parents were not the role models needed to allow the children to identify with strong, truly adult men or women. The children's children also suffer from having the same kinds of infantile parents. Custody battles are excellent ways to guarantee infantile responses in both battling parents, often continuing long after the war is over. This then guarantees prolonged childlike behavior in the kids who are deprived of appropriate role models for good growth and maturity.

Note that *both* marital partners are subject to this type of problem. Most people automatically think of the wife as the individual who remains dependent on her husband, even in these supposedly liberated days. However, wives have no monopoly on this behavior; husbands can be just as dependent, even if that dependency is not expressed as financial dependency. Emotional dependence on a mothering figure can be even greater than financial dependence. Certainly, it can create greater problems. In the popular literature, husbands who are jealous of their children are as much a cliché as wives who cling to their husbands for the sake of being supported.

A whole spectrum of different needs for the other spouse can be present in any of the individuals who cling to unrewarding marriages. The dependency states described are only the most commonly seen. Each person has his or her own deeply personal reasons which are generally unconscious. Significantly, a whole spectrum of similar needs may underlie the necessity to fight for the children after divorce.

The idea that parents may depend on their children may not be familiar. Obviously, we automatically perceive that children depend on their parents, and we do not generally recognize that the forces may go in the opposite direction as well. It is often for the sake of fulfilling those dependency needs, also unconscious and unknown to the people who may have them, that many custody battles are instituted and fought, and they result in dreadful experiences for the children.

These questions are directed to all parents:

- What kind of relationship did your own parents have?

  — Did they stick together?
  — Why or why not?
  — Do you ever find yourself acting like one or both of them?
  — Do you think that you might also act like either of them insofar as your attitudes toward marriage and children are concerned?
  — Is that good for you? For your children?
  — Was it good for your marriage?

Parents and Changing Sex Roles

I hear people ask, "How can parents depend on their children—and for what?" Obviously, when children are young they are not likely to be the sources of financial reward for a family unless they are performers. Fortunately, there are very few child performers around, and most of them do not make that much money anyway. Of course, children can be seen as breadwinners of a sort if a considerable settlement is placed on them or if considerable child support is provided. But these situations are rare. If the parents are not dependent on the children for money, then what is it?

Perhaps some examples can help clarify this puzzling issue. The first which comes to mind is the need for parents to be parents simply to fulfill their own senses of identity. In my practice, I have seen many fathers who have not felt sufficiently secure in their roles as men, and the presence of their children for them attests to their capacity to be fathers and, therefore, to be men. The impression of many of my colleagues is that more of these cases will be seen because of the threats posed to many insecure men by the women's movement.

The emerging independence of women has led to many

responses among men, not all of them encouraging. Many men simply cannot respond appropriately to the emerging assertiveness of women. They have not had sufficient experience to be sure that their positions are not really threatened as much as they fear. The anxiety felt by the men who respond so negatively may well lead to fears that their manhood itself may be threatened. That fear, of course, really represents a deep, unconscious fear, probably present since childhood, which can best be expressed as the idea that their manhood—a man's own image of his own masculinity and his feelings about it—is threatenable.

I am reminded of one patient, a 30-year-old man who was rearing his children as a single parent. It was not until well into the therapy sessions, begun because of his depression, that he was able to verbalize that he really wanted custody of the children because of what the children could bring him. He was not referring to the idealized joys of fatherhood here. Instead, he felt that the children could bring him into contact with women who might then be attracted to him because of his attentiveness to the children. It was obvious that he did not feel sufficiently secure about his own ability to attract women who could represent potential relationships for him. He had really been wounded by the divorce and even more by his wife's finding someone else. He really lacked the sense of identity required to overcome that blow, despite success in business and on the athletic field. He felt that his wife had left him because of his supposed deficiency as a male, which definitely prevented him from perceiving himself as attractive. He became dependent on his children to compensate for that supposed deficiency.

If we think that men have it tough in responding to the women's movement, we must also look at what is happening to women. Think of the pressures they are under, with the expectations of the family members who reared them a generation ago now conflicting with current expectations. Identity problems abound in today's women, originally taught that the highest values are those of domestic life and motherhood. The women's movement has preached many lessons which indicate that motherhood may actually be a hindrance to the fulfillment of a woman's life. The rhetoric of the new movement has often been inflammatory, and even Betty Friedan, one of its original leaders, has recently written that much of the thrust of the women's movement may have been antichild (*The Second Stage*, New York, Summit Books, 1981).

A woman reared to promote domestic virtues may well see herself as incapable of being the type of person idealized by the liberation movement. The demands on the liberated woman are considerable. New responsibilities in the economic and other arenas will, of course, lead to even more new demands. Many women have yet to learn that they can fulfill those demands. They can be excused. After all, they were not taught that they could. They may even have been taught that it was not ladylike to try to meet them.

Keeping the children following the divorce may be a way many women avoid the demands of the movement. By maintaining the identity of motherhood, they may well cling to that which they feel they can do more comfortably, avoiding the demands of assertiveness. Of course, when fighting for one's child, assertiveness is a valued trait, and one which is not to be put down. But is that assertiveness really for a good cause if the motivation for keeping the children has less to do with the welfare of the children than with one's own welfare?

These days, with the economic crunch and its resultant problems, women who elect to keep their children may well find themselves having to enter the job market anyway. That may make them less liberated than bound, since it is often harder for them than for the men who may have been the breadwinners during the marriages. Many women have not had the job experiences or the training to compete for jobs in the open market. Nonetheless, they may well have to compete because there will not be enough money forthcoming in these inflated times from their ex-husbands. Alimony or spousal support by any other name is becoming a relic of the past, not seen very often in today's society except among the very wealthy. The need for mothers to work should, by rights, urge them to ensure that their ex-husbands maintain their relationships with their children. This would tend to make life easier for mothers, who could then count on fathers to relieve them on occasion. Often, though, the very fact that they have to work creates even more resentment, and that resentment in turn creates a climate within which such continued relationships become very difficult.

Other women determine that they are going to enter the larger arena via the portal provided by the women's movement. They decide that they are not going to seek custody of their children, a decision which meshes well with the newly found capacities of many men to serve as both father and mother to young children. I have known a number of women who have done that and who have maintained excellent contact with their children who were being reared by their ex-husbands. Some of those women really shared quality time with their children, providing them with solid and affecting relationships. I have also known a number of women who did not respond that way and who instead saw their children less and less. Some of them rationalized, though, about quality time, as have some men I have known.

The decision to sacrifice custody for the liberated sphere is not made easily by most women, despite the hostile attitudes of observers who are mostly male. Guilt is provoked in women regardless of which direction they choose. If they wish to proceed with their domestic responsibilities, women's activist groups may call them cowards or worse. If they choose to lessen the demands of the mother role by not seeking custody, their own parents and other family members will probably give them a bad time. The world still has a generally punitive attitude toward women who do not rear their children. After all, it is reasoned, if she did not get custody of the kids, there must be something wrong with her. If he did not get custody—well, that's only to be expected!

These questions are for mothers:

• How will you pursue a career if you have custody of the children?

— Will you need to learn a career from the bottom up?
— Will the career necessitate odd hours, including nights?
— Will you be able to count on the reliability of the help you have arranged to watch over the children?

• Can you make your career goals and methods into something positive between you and your children?

— Are you defensive about it?
— Do you *really* devote all the time you can to the children?
— Do you communicate with them about your work and your goals?
— Are they proud of you? Are you proud of yourself?

Resentment and Dependency

The extended withdrawal of one parent following the separation hurts children terribly. So does the prolonged preoccupation of the custodial parent of either sex with the struggles of renewed and unfamiliar single life, including single parenthood. Any other problems that result from the divorce, if continued for long times, present drastic threats to the children. But, of all these, the manipulative expression of rage toward the opposing spouse by either or both parents hurts the children the most. That rage is fueled even more by the difficult experiences of single parenthood.

Every marriage counseling service which attempts to deal with the problems of divorce and custody has a collection of clients, men and women, who display a strange type of dependency on their children because the children serve as a conduit to the other parent. Sometimes the conduit is there for the needy spouse to continue at least some kind of a relationship with the estranged spouse. The dependency, of course, is really on the other spouse, but there is an associated dependency on the children, who allow for the real dependency on the other spouse to be fulfilled, at least to some degree. Sometimes the needed relationship is carried on by the battles between the spouses. Often the real purpose of those constant fights is to continue the relationship in some form or other, even though the battlers are not aware of this.

In other instances, the rage is so tremendous in one or both parents that a dependency develops on the children because they serve as a negative conduit. Instead of allowing for a shred of a fantasied positive relationship between the estranged parents, they serve as an excuse for the parents to vent their spleens at one another. They really do not want the children as much as they want to get back at each other for the difficulties which led to the breakup or for the hurt of the breakup itself. That type of dependency on children might be the most harmful—it not only ensures that the children will have infantile parents throughout their lives, it also provides them with an atmosphere of constant hostility.

Prolonged and repeated custody battles often germinate in that need to vent resentment. Some observers, mostly lawyers, have stated that those types of suits may actually be benefiting the parents by providing court activity which allows for formalized venting. They are the only kinds of custody battles which should wind up in court, *if* the judge can do something to stop the mutual provocation. I have known some courageous judges who have taken some extreme steps to ensure the cessation of the counter-provocations. In some cases, they have actually removed the children from the custodial household if they determined that the custodial parent was the provoking one. They did not, however, automatically change custody to the other parent if it was felt unwise to do so. In other cases, they have jailed the noncustodial parent if they determined that he or she was the provoking one.

I have known cases in which provoking parents were actually encouraged by their attorneys to continue to be provocative to exhaust the other parent, who might then give up the battle and also give up the children. The lawyers assured their clients that they did not have to fear any charges of contempt of court for provoking again. They told their clients that family court judges do not press contempt-of-court charges against parents because they fear that doing so will affect the children badly. Take this warning seriously—some judges have put those parents in jail for contempt.

In the cases I have known, the jailed parents were all noncustodial fathers. The sentence was passed in the face of pleas by the attorneys that jail would prevent the fathers from working and therefore paying child support. The judge, knowing that the attorney would try to use that ploy, ignored it. The jail sentences were brief but obviously effective, and the fathers were able to keep their jobs. They also continued paying child support, and, for the most part, they discontinued their inappropriate attempts to gain custody.

Judges have also told me that they are now considering placing problem mothers in jail, too. They reason that this will not harm the children any more than the problems stimulated by mothers who provoke legal battles. The judges are probably right.

In the cases I have known, sentencing a parent for contempt of court was helpful. It not only stopped the recurrent battle, it stopped the attorneys from the heinous practice of putting children through hell to satisfy their clients' wishes.

——— · ———

The Absolutely Last Resort

After all my warnings about custody battles, and after all my cautions indicating that they must be avoided, I now feel a little like the captain of the *HMS Pinafore*, who, after a series of, "No, never's," admits that he really *hardly ever* gets sick at sea. I now have to address the fact that there are probably times when custody battles must be fought. But I make that admission only grudgingly. It is really hardly ever.

When should a concerned parent seek legal help to gain custody of a child? The indications for this are few and far between. The main reason must center about the *fact* (not the suspicion but the fact) that the other parent's contacts with the child have been *demonstrated* to be definitely harmful to the child. Demonstration implies more than getting some half-baked expert to testify that, in his or her opinion, continued contact with that parent will probably be harmful. Abuse by parents will be discussed in a later chapter, but this represents the major cause for legitimate custody fights. But the abuse must be demonstrated, and the harmful effects on the child must also be demonstrated. Predictions of possible abuse and of possible harm via possible abuse are inadequate bases for these battles.

Severe mental illness in one parent may be adequate reason for the other parent to seek custody, but this might be for only a limited time. A temporary change of custody might be more appropriate under some circumstances. Fortunately, psychiatric treatments of major mental illnesses are more effective these days than before, and parents who have had breakdowns can recover. The cases mentioned earlier which discussed parents who were alcoholics or even prostitutes are good examples of situations in which judges felt that the relationships between those parents and their children should not be discontinued despite the parents' problems. Even in cases of psychosis in a parent, the child ought to reconstitute a relationship with him or her when the parent is well enough to maintain control and to visit profitably with the child. In Chapter 6 (dealing with parental abuse) you will read that many families enter treatment as a whole, keeping the contacts between children and abusing parents uninterrupted. Those cases have the potential of turning out well.

So, even if custody is won on the basis of the other parent being unfit because of abusive trends or severe illness, the custodial parent will need to think seriously about allowing the child to continue the relationship with the other parent. The child will continue to need both parents regardless of the situation. If visitation (to be discussed in a later chapter) can be supervised and constructive, the custodial parent should encourage it. The child will need it.

———— · ————

Numerous motivations can underlie the decisions to seek custody of children following divorce, and those motivations certainly may not lie within the conscious awareness of the people doing the fighting. This remains true despite the sometimes pious pronouncements of the parents who say that they are fighting for the children for noble reasons. To recapitulate, the motivations are representations in many cases of unconscious needs for the children, and those needs may also cover up even more basic needs for the estranged spouse.

Surprisingly enough, the fulfillment of those needs might lead to a situation which may be appropriate for the children, even though the battle may not be fought with that end in mind. It is possible that, accidentally, the children may actually wind up with the parent who can better take care of them and who can better provide for their needs, including making sure that they have unimpeded access to the other parent. For example, if the custodial parent remains emotionally dependent on his or her ex-spouse, the custodial parent will make sure that the children see the other parent so that he or she can, too.

Although in some instances some good can come from the

type of emotional handicaps we have studied here, remember that these effects of a custody battle are accidental, incidental, second-hand, and definitely not geared to the best interests of the children as much as to the best interests of the dependent parent. In too many situations, though, the actual welfare of the children may be sacrificed to the fulfillment of unknown needs of the battling parent. That is what is usually seen in battles over custody, and it is certainly to the detriment of the children. If you persist in inappropriate attempts to fight battles for the custody of your children, you may find that it is to your detriment too. Think very hard about it.

CHAPTER 4

— . . . —

What's a Parent to Do?

If you're going through it, you already know better than I that there is very little fair about the breakup of a marriage. Chapters 2 and 3 were devoted to the most important commandment of divorce: *Thou shalt not fight over the kids and drag them through a custody battle.* Because so little is fair elsewhere, I shall try to be fair by devoting some space to the "thou shalts" as well. If you must not fight a custody battle, it is only fair that I tell you what you *should* do.

You Must Talk:
Then You Must Talk Some More

The most important thing to do is to discuss and eventually agree with your spouse about what to do with the children. This is not an idealized instruction, uttered from an ivory tower. I know that it is often very difficult to talk with an ex-spouse or, even harder, with a still-divorcing one. The mutual anger and hurt too often get in the way of any serious discussion, and attempts at conversation often turn into shouting matches, if not worse.

To that, I say, "Whoa!" Be mad at each other, but don't be mad at the kids. It is really possible to do that. As during any war, eventually the warring parties will have to sit down with each other and discuss a peace treaty. If they could do this earlier instead of later, many lives and much property would be saved. During the late, terrible Viet Nam conflict, I saw a number of divorcing parents who marched in protest parades but who would not confer with their divorcing spouses. They insisted that the opposing governments sit down at a peace conference, but they would not sit down with their divorcing husbands or wives! It is easy to point fingers elsewhere and very hard to reflect on one's own behavior. Just as in any war, however, sitting down with your divorcing wife or husband will save your children's lives and also will save considerable property.

Sometimes it helps to do this with the aid of a third party or even with the aid of both attorneys if they have already been consulted and if they are amenable. Some are. Popular mythology and prejudice to the contrary, not all attorneys work to make cases more complicated. Many are quite helpful; they go out of their way to aid the battling spouses to communicate at least enough to prevent an all-out custody fight. Friends who serve as objective or dispassionate third parties are rarer, but I have known of cases in which they have done yeoman service as combination consolers and Dutch uncles, even outshouting the battlers and forcing them into positions of mutual recognition. You may not want to risk losing such good friends though. If you're divorcing, you probably will feel a need to keep them.

Sometimes it helps for one spouse to write a letter to the divorcing spouse, pointing out his or her wish to discuss the future of the children and to keep them and their disposition out of the divorce conflict. Writing is nearly always better—certainly easier—than trying to talk whenever the emotional level is too strong. No matter how the attempt might be made to get the other spouse to sit down and talk about the children, the necessity is there to do it, even in the eye of the tornado.

In some cases, I have suggested that both parties sign an informal agreement that they will not fight over the disposition of the children, and that they will each work to see that the children continue to receive the love of both parents. Further, they will each be on guard against any interference by themselves or by anyone else which will adversely affect easy, warm, and profitable contact with the children by each parent. By and large, such informal agreements spell out the decision made by both parents that they will continue to assume the responsibility of being parents to their children, even though they have determined that they can no longer assume responsibility for each other. Most important, such agreements spell out that each parent wants the other parent to continue assuming that responsibility.

Once again, I must emphasize that these agreements can be, and actually are, worked out more easily than you might think between divorcing spouses. I have often seen how possible problems affecting the children can be nipped in the bud by one parent sitting down with the other parent, or by writing, or by somehow coming to a mutual decision. *It can be done, and it is done,* even with people who remain very angry at each other.

Such agreements represent self-determined joint custody decisions of the best kind. The best kind are those hammered out by the parents out of a sense of continued responsibility and good will toward the children. To hell with each other, maybe, but not with the children! The worst kind of joint custody decisions are those directed by courts in cases where the parents are not able to communicate enough with each other to recognize their joint responsibilities toward the kids. The courts may wish or even think that their directives will force the parents to do just that, but more often than not they do not succeed, and the children only suffer more.

———— . ————

These questions are for divorcing parents:

- How do you talk with your divorcing spouse?
- Can you control your anger? How do you deal with it?

— Do you tell the other person frankly that you're mad?
— Does your ex do the same to you?
— How does your ex respond to you?
— Does acknowledging the anger of both parties allow easier talking about people neither of you are mad at, such as the children?
— Do you soften his/her erupting anger by recognizing it but not rising to the bait or not responding in kind?
— In contrast, do you really revel in your anger? (Be honest.)

More About Joint Custody: When and How and Why It Works

I have commented on joint custody in earlier chapters: it is an extremely important issue and needs further elaboration and understanding. Many people do not understand joint custody, even some judges who order it and some counselors who advise it.

You may recall my observation that many people think of joint custody as a situation in which each parent has equal time with the children—this is probably the most common misconception about joint custody.

———— . ————

Time is joint custody's least important aspect. Ongoing, mutual responsibility for the children is its most important aspect. Joint custody really has nothing to do with where the children live or, actually, how often or how long each parent sees them. It has everything to do with the children's opportunity and encouragement to see each parent and to have each parent as a continuing influence in their lives.

———— · ————

I have seen joint custody work very well when the parents were separated by a continent. I have seen it fail dismally when the parents continued to live close to each other, even when they continued to move in and out of the same house every week or so.

Joint custody has even more definitions than does marital happiness! Also, many terms are used which mean joint custody. Just as one example, people sometimes talk about shared custody. Perhaps the idea goes down easier that way. It is probably harder to think in terms of joint responsibility. Sharing is nicer, and having custody of something may sound preferable to having responsibility for it. Other synonyms for joint custody include divided custody, alternating custody, and coparenting or shared parenting.

There are many ways to set up joint custody and still have it mean that both parents continue to share responsibility for the children. Responsibility for children is a heavy burden in the best of situations, even in intact families. After divorce, it becomes heavier. Sometimes it gets so heavy that one or even both parents find themselves unable to maintain their commitments, and one or even both may withdraw from their children. Assuming the continuing obligation for the physical, medical, financial, educational, emotional, and all the other needs of the children is a commitment made when people decide to have children. It is also a commitment reaffirmed by making a joint custody decision.

If parents can no longer follow through with those commitments, they must attempt to make alternate plans which allow others—even the hated ex-spouse—to assume the responsibility for their children. But divorce itself ought not to mean that one parent automatically can no longer continue the obligation to his or her own children. For example, even though many fights after divorce are about the failure of the ex-spouse (usually the father) to make child support payments regularly to the spouse who has physical custody of the children, experience shows that the money is the least of the problems affecting the delinquent parent. When payments are withheld, the reason may not have anything to do with a shortage of money. The holding back often represents other conflicts. In fact, the financial responsibilities of a parent to a child probably are the easiest to tolerate. Writing a check may be tough in financially tough times, but it is not emotionally wrenching.

It takes a lot of fiber to continue to go to see one's own kids at times prescribed by someone else in a home that is no longer one's own and is perhaps occupied by someone taking his or her place with the ex-spouse. There are reasons behind the dreadful statistic that 40 percent of fathers lose effective contact with their children after divorce, and they are not all centered about the fact that he's a real bastard, as so many ex-wives allege! Parents who continue their relationships with their children in the face of emotionally wracking conditions deserve a lot of credit.

I have already alluded to the method of joint custody whereby the parents each move in and out of a home in which the children stay. That arrangement has been rather piquantly described as a "bird's nest," by Dr. Anthony Atwell of Stanford University. But it often is not as sweet as implied by the words of the old song, "A little nest of robins where the roses bloom . . ." I doubt very much that I, personally, could move in and out like that, but if the parents *who have agreed to do it* can do so successfully, more power to them. Most important, if the children tolerate this type of relationship well without developing even more problems, more power to them too.

The only criterion for the success of *mutually agreed-on* joint custody is the ongoing welfare of the children. If the children tolerate their parents moving in and out, fine. I have known of cases in which this was successful. I have also known cases in which this was unsuccessful because of the strain placed on the parents and on the children. Parents moving in and out are often under great pressure because of that instability. In turn, this can place terrific pressures on children. Remember, anxiety is more catching than the measles. The children may also feel increased anxiety because they often become caught again in their parents' unresolved disagreements, sometimes made worse by the frequency of the parental moves. But if it works well for all concerned, fine! That's the bottom line.

I have also known cases in which younger children travel back and forth to their respective parents' different homes, usually on a weekly or biweekly basis. I have known of even more cases in which children travel back and forth to their respective parents' different homes on the basis of staying in one house during the school year and in the other when school is out during vacations and holidays. Judges and other authorities sometimes express concern that frequent moves back and forth can be confusing and disruptive, especially to younger children. This may be so, but it cannot be predicted. Often the benefits of assured relationships with each parent outweigh any possible inconveniences.

———— · ————

The key to all these successful formats is that, regardless of where the children or the parents are or who does the moving, the children must always have stress-free access to and communication with each parent. Each parent encourages the children to contact the other parent, and, in fact, promises to contact the other whenever something special comes up. That is successful joint custody.

———— · ————

It makes no difference if one parent has actual physical custody of the kids for far longer than the other parent or if the other parent does not assume physical custody at all but, instead, visits freely with the children. As Dr. Elissa Benedek, of the University of Michigan, has said, the important issue is that the children spend *substantial* time with each parent. The definition of substantial may differ from case to case insofar as the length of time is concerned, but it ought not differ insofar as the quality of that time is concerned. That is what joint custody and joint responsibility are all about, and that is what you must strive for with your children. Remember, too, that the arrangements can represent successful, real joint custody even if the judge has not ordered that by name. Joint custody can probably be defined more effectively by parents than by a judge, as long as they adhere to the concept of genuine, substantial quality time.

If joint custody is mutually agreed on, time spent with each parent, even if one is actually a visiting parent, should be handled such that the parent expresses real interest in the children and their activities and encourages them. As an example, if the parent who has most of the physical custody has to suffer through the violin practicing, the other joint custodial or shared custodial parent should at least share the responsibility by suffering through the recital. No, the divorced parents do not have to sit together or, for that matter, even communicate with each other in the audience if they continue to find that difficult. Arrangements should be made beforehand, and it is probably best if the parent who sees the child less often takes him or her out for the ritual ice cream after the artistic triumph, but these are issues of visitation and dealing with the children which will be discussed in detail later.

Often, when parents cannot agree about their children during marriage, they may be forced into a position of having to pay lip service to agreeing about them after they are divorced. The judge will spell out rules and regulations regarding custody and responsibility, visitation, domicile, and all the

other matters which the parents should have decided themselves.

———— · ————

Please try to do your own, mutual deciding. That is the
paramount "thou shalt!" It really makes it much easier
for all concerned, you and the kids.

———— · ————

In contrast, an order stating that the parents will do certain
things, even though it is signed by the judge, does not mean
that those things will be done. One or both parents may continue to fight with the other about one of or all the arrangements. One parent may withdraw, leaving the other parent as
the one with, in effect, sole custody. The children will lose out
by not having any relationship with the other parent.

Whatever happens, if the result is not troublesome to the
parent with more responsibility for the children, the judge will
probably not hear about it. That parent will not complain or
seek legal help. The judge may make an order mandating joint
custody and never hear from the couple again. The judge will
believe that his or her order solved the problem and that the
parents and children are doing well obeying it. This is one
reason that joint custody orders have become so popular. The
illusion is gained that people obey them. But of course, the
opposite may be true. The parents may continue to fight, or
one parent may withdraw. In any case, the kids will suffer.

As mentioned, joint custody decisions are becoming increasingly popular. In fact, in many states, the law says that
joint custody is the preferable mode of deciding the disposition
of the children of divorce. Sometimes the law goes even further, stating that this type of disposition is mandated in all
cases, even contested ones, unless there are specific contraindi-
cations to it. Joint custody has become a fad imposed by many
well-intended judges and court counselors. When it is in agreement with the wishes of the parents, it works well. In those

situations, though, there really is no need for any decision from the bench about what should happen to the children. When the parents are not able to use it, the results are often disastrous, because the joint custody decision actually empowers the parents to continue to fight if they feel that their rights are being infringed.

If the parents continue to fight, the judges hear about it because one or the other parent will usually recontact the lawyer, and more courtroom battles will result. However, if one parent withdraws, the other one rarely goes to court about it. In fact, he or she is often grateful for the withdrawal—it may be less troublesome than enforced communication or contact. But the judges, hearing nothing from them, believing that everything is always working by virtue of their orders, will continue to order the same things. They will continue to believe in the efficacy of imposed joint custody, completely unaware of the failures which do not come before their eyes. It is better to do your own ordering.

———— . ————

The following questions are directed to fathers who do not have custody of their children:

- How are you dealing with a real inability to keep up the payments for child and spousal support?

  — Is the inability *really* real?
  — If not, how are you dealing with any feelings you might have about the children?
  — Do you think that they are suffering at all because of the nonpayment?
  — If the inability to pay is real, does your ex-wife understand?
  — Have you tried to reach an understanding with her, or have you withdrawn?

———— . ————

Getting Help to Talk

Let us return to the topic of communicating with each other about the kids as you are splitting up. Tears, rage, nausea, vomiting, sleeplessness, all follow marital breakups. I am well aware that the ability or even the wish to sit down and talk is hard to find within yourselves at those times. In general, sitting down to talk is way down on the priority scale, probably well below the impulse to run over the opposing spouse with a heavy truck, but, if you have kids, they will remind you that you ought to talk. If the kids stay with you as mother, or if the mother leaves and they stay with you as father, or if either one of you leave and take the children with you, they will remind you in any case. They will wonder about the other parent and about their household. They will ask to see the other parent. At least they will ask unless they recognize that asking for their other parent results in rage on your part. They don't want to make you rageful; they have enough trouble as it is.

Families are generally helpful to divorcing parents. Sometimes they may be critical and rejecting, especially if they have been that way earlier in life. More often than not, though, they can be counted on to provide at least a modicum of emotional support. Going home to Mama and Daddy is not just an old joke. There may be no place else to go, especially if the grandparents are needed to help with the kids. My experience is that the grandparents usually work to get the divorcing couple to talk, even though they may approach the topic gingerly. The grandparents have one advantage. They usually discuss the situation with their own friends who may have gone through the same traumas with their own children, and they are often more easily influenced by those horror stories. Their friends tell different stories than the friends of the divorcing couple.

The grandparents may not want to hurt their son or daughter by appearing disloyal, but they usually respond to the misery of their grandchildren. However, their sensitivity to the grandchildren can be a two-edged sword, causing them to respond inappropriately to the marital breakup. For example, I have never known any grandparents who were not frightened of the possibility of losing their grandchildren because of the divorces of their children. Although there are many instances of grandparents backing up the custody battles of their own children in misguided attempts to secure their own continued relationships with the grandchildren, more grandparents probably serve to prevent the battles in the long run.

Friends could serve the same purpose, but my experience is that friends are not listened to as well as parents in the midst of the initial stages of the breakup. Marital breakups always cause some regression and fear in the partners, and in such instances the divorcing spouses may revert to childlike relationships with their own parents. If the parents are good parents and do not derive satisfaction from having their children depend on them again, they will guide their children into adulthood once again, pointing them in the direction of thinking about their own children. However, when friends are contacted, if they are good friends it is likely that they will say little if anything. Probably they will simply listen and provide the necessary shoulders to cry on. Later on, though, there may be an opportunity for them to inject the idea that the kids ought to be thought about, unless the friends are preoccupied with their own divorces and the problems they are having with and about their own children. It is quite an epidemic!

Of course, it also sometimes happens that the divorcing parent can think about the kids without any urges from an outside party. If so, that parent is to be congratulated for possessing the requisite degree of maturity to proceed with what has to be done. If, in the eye of the tornado, a parent can think about his or her kids without prompting, that parent ought to be able to sit on his or her feelings and control them at least enough to open up the subject with the other spouse. Perhaps it is too bad that you, as that parent, might be the one who may have to bear that burden of responsibility for the children's welfare, but I opened this chapter by pointing out that little is fair in the breakup of a marriage. Fair or not, I must depend on you to do most of the work here.

The important issue is always the goal. If the goal is to open contact with the other parent in order to fight, then nothing will be accomplished. The other parent may not be able to discuss any issues, including the children, quietly. There may be too much rage, even if that other parent is the one who left or who instituted the separation. But the parent with the capacity to think about the kids has the capacity to refuse to rise to the bait tossed by the other parent. If, as has been said elsewhere, a soft answer turneth away wrath, a soft answer must be given at all times. *Give a little* for the kids' sakes.

The rage can get out of control at times. When it does, tragedy is the usual result. In my own city, during the time I was writing this book, an enraged, estranged father killed his children's new stepfather. Do I have to tell you that the issue was the custody of the children? The father came over to the children's new home, argued with their new stepfather, fought with him, and then shot him. I have no idea why the father had been denied custody, but I have a hunch that he had also been denied other access to the children as well. When rage is already starting to boil in a divorce, raising the flame under it by fighting about the children and by preventing free and open contact will usually lead to some kind of disaster, although, thankfully, most often not to one like this. I can only wonder sadly about the children involved in that case. What will they think of their father and of themselves? What are the mother's feelings, and how will they affect the children?

I am not a soft-headed idealist. I know that there are times when it is impossible to communicate across a table. But I know of no time when it is not appropriate to try like hell to do so. If attempts at face-to-face discussion fail, I urge parents to write their ideas about their children to their spouses. I always warn them, though, to keep copies of that carefully worded, carefully edited, and probably rewritten letter. Later, it may be handy or even necessary to refer to it if all attempts at resolving the issues of the children have failed.

If it comes to that, both lawyers will need to know what has been originally suggested, and certainly the court will be interested in any genuine constructive attempts made by either party to resolve the issue of the disposition of the children. You should be warned, though. Keeping the copy of the letter may not only benefit the writer. I have seen cases in which the writer later changes his or her mind, deciding to become less conciliatory and less willing to share the responsibility for the children as the other parent becomes increasingly open. The letters then become valuable for the opposition. They may also become valuable for the counselor who then enters the scene, attempting to intervene in this dreadful situation.

———— · ————

These questions are for all divorcing parents:

• How are your parents taking your divorce? How do you want them to take it?

— Do you want them to provide emotional support for you?
— To do that, do they have to hate your ex-spouse?
— Are they more afraid of losing your grandchildren than of losing you?
— If so, how does that make you feel?
— Is that feeling helpful? What does it do to the relationship between you and them?

• How are your ex-spouse's parents taking the divorce? Are you in touch with them? Are they in touch with you? Do you want them to back you, too? Do you resent their backing their son or daughter?

Counseling and Mediation

I have not said much thus far about counseling during divorce, although it is a subject of enormous importance. I hope that both parents will talk with each other so that counselors will not be needed, at least about decisions affecting the children. I hope that the divorcing parents will come to a working and workable agreement about how and where the children will live and that each parent will encourage continued contact between the children and the other parent. Doing so will be of enormous benefit to the kids and to the parents as well. Counseling, though, plays an increasingly frequent role in divorce. In fact, just like joint custody, in many jurisdictions it is the law that divorcing couples must seek counseling by some professionals before any divorce decree is granted. Sometimes the counseling is necessary only when the disposition of the children is involved. California was the first state to enact legislation calling for mandatory mediation in cases of contested custody, and the practice of mediation in divorce has grown enormously throughout the entire country.

Mediation has become a buzz word. Again like joint custody, it appears to be defined in as many ways as the number of people who use the term. I don't know how to define it except in terms of counseling, but, by and large, the concept centers around the recognized need for a divorcing couple to come to some mutual decision or compromise about each of their individual wishes. The theory is that negotiation can be carried on by an objective third party such that both combatants will necessarily recognize that they will have to give a little. It makes enormous sense. All of us realize that each of the warring spouses will have to give up at least a little, perhaps even a lot, if a judge makes an arbitrary decision about their children, their property, or their lives. I suppose that mediation is really what I have been preaching in this book, even if a third party is unnecessary and the couple do this on their own.

A warning is very necessary here. Enforced mediation may

be a problem, depending on who does it. Private so-called mediation clinics have sprung up like mushrooms across the land. In many states and in all Canadian provinces, conciliation courts or otherwise-named court clinics are also available to deal with marital disputes in attempts to get them resolved before the judges have to do it. The counselors in many of these court-associated clinics are well-trained and experienced social workers or psychologists, or even probation or child-protective officers. My experience with many of these clinics is that they are helpful. My experience with many others, and with some private mediation agencies, is that they are not. In fact, they can be harmful.

According to the Los Angeles *Times* (July 6, 1983), the president of the (then) 1200-member Academy of Family Mediators predicted that half the divorces in the United States will be mediated, not litigated, within 5 years. I will be the first to agree that it will be very helpful to divorcing couples to mediate their differences instead of fighting them out in court. Time and money will be saved, and considerable emotional pain will be avoided if mediation succeeds. But mediation must be wanted by the couple for it to succeed when carried on by the majority of the people who now call themselves professional mediators. Experience has shown that those couples who continue to insist on fighting and who cannot sit down voluntarily across a conference table without continuing to fight, are beyond the expertise of most of those counselors.

At this time there are no quality controls affecting the level of competence of mediators. I have already mentioned one mediation organization, and there are many others; my impression is that there is little impetus for standard setting among them. A certificate in mediation can be obtained by taking a 7-day course advertised by one of the associations. Other advertisements offer even shorter courses. Professor Jay Folberg of the Lewis and Clark Law School in Portland, Oregon, and past chairperson of the American Bar Association's family law section on mediation and arbitration, said in the Los

Angeles *Times* (July 6, 1983) that "Training is really a farce. Courses are not monitored and are mostly money-making efforts. To say you're a trained mediator is to say you're putting out money for it." Even more pointedly, in the same article, Hugh McIsaac, director of the Family Mediation and Conciliation Services of the Los Angeles Superior Court, commented, "It's an insane situation. There are some very effective mediators, and others who have taken a five-day course and put up a shingle. . . ."

Even well-trained people can make mistakes, especially if they are loaded with cases and have little time to deal adequately with each case. The rush and congestion in the court clinics is proportional to the divorce rate. Another problem with many of the court clinics is the use to which they are put by some judges. I have known a number of instances in which judges have praised clinic workers to the skies just because they have kept the cases from having to be tried before them, thereby relieving their own docket congestion. The judges may fail to realize (I hope that it is not a case of their not caring) that clinic workers may be imposing their will arbitrarily on the confused and frightened couple without an adequate investigation, insisting on a solution which may not represent the best interests of the child in question and which may be impossible for the parents to carry through.

An exceptionally flagrant example of this practice occurred when a very strong and demanding conciliation court worker insisted that the couple accept joint physical custody of their 4-month-old baby, *who was being breast-fed by the mother.* Joint custody is one thing; joint physical custody is another and it obviously makes uninterrupted breast feeding impossible. Even the La Leche League, an international organization promoting breast feeding, became involved in that case, which, as could be predicted, found its way into court. Fortunately, the judge was more sensitive and perceptive than the very arbitrary conciliation court worker.

Although that example is extreme and represents a generalized failure of sensitivity or even of common sense at just about any level, it is true that many people staffing these clinics or otherwise setting themselves up as mediators may have little, if any, training in child development or child diagnosis. Often they do not even see the children for more than short times, if they see them at all. Even if they have some background in child psychology, their case loads may prevent their being able to use that knowledge effectively. They attempt to evaluate each of the parents for comparative fitness, but in so doing they may not take into consideration the special or particular needs of the children.

I have already commented that mediation for divorcing couples who want to mediate can be valuable and helpful. My own experience in observing mediation in many locales in this country and in Canada leads me to conclude that there really ought to be two types of mediators, with two separate standards. Those who deal with voluntary couples who want to mediate do not really have to be as well-trained in the techniques of psychotherapy and other interventions, or, for that matter, in child development. But the mediators to whom warring couples are sent when they refuse to come to any mutual decision about anything, whether it is the children or any other disputed issue, must be far more professionally advanced. Those warring couples are beyond the reach of any quick-course mediator.

Conciliation courts or court clinics are as good as the people staffing them and the case load allow them to be. The same can be said about the newly burgeoning mediation clinics—and honesty insists that I say the same thing about private psychologists and psychiatrists as well. Even they make mistakes, or perform only perfunctory evaluations at times. Keep this in mind when considering decisions affecting the children—long before the time comes for a referral to mandatory mediators, whoever they may be or however well trained. As parents, you have more time, more of an emotional investment, and more background regarding your children than any expert, *and you have the ability to reach mutual decisions about them.* At the least, you can develop the ability if you decide to set aside the rage for a little while. The decisions you reach about your children will most likely be kept. So many externally imposed decisions are not.

Do not make yourselves into those difficult cases which resist voluntary mediation if, in fact, you need mediation at all because you have not been able to do it all yourselves. Becoming a difficult, involuntary case means that you have already made it tougher on yourself than you need to, and, even worse, you have made it tougher on your kids. The fact that you have made it tougher for the mediators may not be as important, unless you get one who is outgunned by your case. This does not mean that those more difficult cases are not amenable to mediation; it simply means that people with more skills and more time to use those skills will need to do the mediating.

———— · ————

These questions are for all divorcing parents:

• How well do you know your mediator?
• How much do you trust him or her?

— Do you see the mediator alone as well as jointly with your divorcing spouse?
— If so, do you tell the mediator things you want kept secret from your divorcing spouse?
— Are they actually kept confidential?
— In that kind of mediation format, should they be kept confidential?
— Is your divorcing spouse telling the mediator the same kinds of secrets?

———— · ————

Lawyers and Mediation

In my practice, I ordinarily deal with difficult cases referred by lawyers or by the courts. I usually do not see divorcing individuals or couples who ask for mediation at the outset. Those folks really do not need me. By the time the divorcing or already-divorced couples see me, they have lawyers of their own and have entered the legal arena. I try to use their lawyers as allies. I speak extensively with them before and after I examine their clients, discussing the case and my viewpoint as an advocate for the children. My experience has been that the lawyers can be very effective in getting their clients to sit down with me and with each other to avoid courtroom hearings.

Lawyers can and do help in other ways as well. I recognize that I do not understand the many legal and other issues associated with child custody in which I am simply not competent: for example, the financial and tax aspects of a marital breakup. I must point out my impression that they are often also beyond the expertise of many divorce lawyers as well. The American Academy of Matrimonial Lawyers, an outstanding educational organization for attorneys, maintains an institute for training its members in tax and many other aspects of law which affect the practice of family law. Most divorce lawyers are not members, however. Nomination to the select Academy is an honor.

Tax and financial issues are very important, not only in the division of property, but also in decisions about who gets the kids and how they will be supported. In California, for example, the *Duke* case has set the precedent that it is possible to predict that children will be harmed emotionally if they are moved from their house after divorce and that property settlements must take that into consideration. The *Duke* ruling has led to many court battles, most of which have been initiated by wives who have been instructed by their attorneys regarding the possible favorable decision that they will be able to keep their houses. Divorce can certainly destroy logical thinking processes. How can middle class couples delude themselves into thinking that a house can be kept and paid for nowadays, after divorce and the establishment of separate households? Besides, kids are harmed far more by physically losing parents than by physically leaving a house if they leave with a loving parent.

In New Jersey, the law states that only lawyers can do divorce mediation. Personally, I find that horrifying, even though I agree that divorcing couples often need lawyers to secure their individual rights. I can only hope that New Jersey lawyers call on other experts for help when they get into issues beyond their expertise. Lawyers are generally not trained in child development, but they may not need to be if they can get their clients to come to a mutual agreement about the disposition of their kids. The lawyers then become as good as the grandparents who might have forced the issue of deciding about the children even earlier.

———— · ————

Recently, during psychotherapy of a young woman in the throes of divorce, I was actually pleased to hear her rageful announcement that she really wanted her two children to grow to hate their father. I was pleased because her telling me indicated that she was becoming increasingly open and honest with herself and with me and that we would be better able to make progress with her depression. That kind of honesty is hard to come by in divorce mediation. It certainly is not likely to come forth spontaneously from most divorcing parents. Once again, we are faced with the nearly universal tendency toward self-delusion. Rage-filled parents will not be able to make peace with those feelings unless they face them honestly. Those feelings may get in the way of resolving the disposition of the children or of allowing the children to rest easily in whatever home they make.

I am not urging psychotherapy for every parent who is being divorced, but I am urging as much self-examination and self-honesty as possible. I urge that all parents try to make peace with their conscious or unconscious goals of having their children hate the other parent. At one time or another most divorcing parents feel that, and making peace with it is a real "thou shalt." If that can be accomplished, the ideal of sitting down across a table and deciding that the two of you can work together about the kids, reserving the right to hate each other's guts about everything else, can become an accomplishment. That will be quality time for the parents. You deserve quality time, too.

CHAPTER 5

· · ·

Monday Mornings: Problems of Visitation

The telephones ring off the hook in most divorce lawyers' offices every Monday morning. The calls are nearly always from resentful or otherwise distraught parents complaining about their ex-spouses who, somehow or other, have screwed up the visitation process. Visiting parents call to complain that the custodial parents do not let the children visit, and custodial parents call to complain about the abuses suffered by their children at the hands of the visiting parents.

Problems of visitation outnumber custody suits. Thus far, most of what has been written here has focused on the problems stimulated by custody battles and the effects of those litigations on the children and the parents who fight over them. It does not soften the effects of those terrible battles to point out that only about 10 or 15 percent of custody cases wind up being disputed in court. Most of the time, fortunately, custody is not disputed, even in these days of increasing awareness by fathers that they, too, can provide excellent and valuable single parenting for their children. When custody is disputed, decisions are generally reached resolving the conflicts before the battling couple goes to court about them. The conflicts are usually resolved on the bases of factors which have nothing to do with the children. Money and other divisions of property usually figure in those peace treaties; 10 or 15 percent do not resolve, and they go to court or to court clinics for attempted resolution.

Disputes over visitation are far more frequent than custody battles. They represent the bread-and-butter of most divorce lawyers' business. Visitation (or, as it is called even more appropriately in Canada and Britain, "access") is the arrangement agreed on by both parents wherein one parent has physical custody of the children and the other parent visits. Visiting does not necessarily mean that the visits are at the home of the custodial parent. In general, the children are picked up there (or at a neutral spot if there is too much residual friction between the parents) and are taken out, perhaps to the visiting parent's home, to his or her family's home, or to Disneyland or a reasonable facsimile.

Courts sometime cling to the outmoded and invalid idea that visiting parents ought not see the children too often because this may disrupt their schedules and may also affect them adversely in other ways. Years ago, courts would often restrict the visits of fathers (they were, and still are, the usual visiting parents) to as little as one day a month and then only to a few hours on that day. Now, with the increasing (but still sometimes grudging) recognition by family court judges that it is healthy for children to see both parents as often as possible, much more liberal visitation is granted in divorce settlements.

In a sense, it is paradoxical that this more liberal attitude developed during the same time that so many judges were influenced by a best-selling text on child custody problems written about a dozen years ago, *Beyond the Best Interests of the Child* (New York, Free Press, 1973). One of the three authors,

Dr. Albert Solnit, is professor of child psychiatry at Yale Medical School. His colleague, Joseph Goldstein, is professor of law at Yale, and the third member of the triumvirate was no less than Anna Freud, daughter of the founder of psychoanalysis and a world-famous child psychoanalyst in her own right. The three combined to write a text which, in part, emphasized their concept of the psychological parent, that natural or appointed adult to whom the child most easily and productively turns for emotional comfort and growth.

Their view, as developed in that influential text, was that the psychological parent is the individual who must regulate the visitation with the other parent or, even more, determine whether such visitation is good for the child and should be carried on at all. They developed that notion because of their experiences with visitation problems which are just as bitterly fought over as custody battles and which also drag the children through emotional mills. The concept of one parent having the authority to choose whether the child sees the other parent, however, is one which sometimes invites overrestriction or no visitation at all, especially if the custodial parent maintains considerable hostility toward the other one and uses his or her power to deprive the visiting parent of any contact with the child. It takes little imagination to visualize how an all-powerful and vindictive parent can use his or her power purely for reasons which have nothing to do with the child's needs but which serve to vent rage toward the other parent.

Parents' rights groups and many others rose up in arms about this idea, and now many judges hesitate to impose this type of solution to a visitation conflict. It often simply provokes appeals to higher courts, and many of those courts have recognized that more contemporary thinking about the best interests of the children recommends contact with both parents—even if the price to be paid is a legal hassle.

As always, though, it makes little difference what the judge decides. If the couple jointly wants the visiting parent to be with the children as much as possible, *and they should,* the couple will make those arrangements. If the visiting member of the parental team feels a need to withdraw from the family, he or she will do so regardless of the court orders and, tragically, regardless of the adverse effect on the youngsters.

———— · ————

The following questions are directed to all divorcing parents:

- Do you believe that a child can have more than one psychological parent?
- If so, do they have to be married or otherwise living together?
- Can separated parents each be psychological parents? Should they be?
- If not, why not? Are your reasons self-serving?

Sources of Visitation Conflicts

Legal battles over visitation are fought by both visiting and custodial parents. Sometimes they are fought by others as well. For example, in a recent California case, grandparents successfully sued to be allowed to visit with their grandchildren. This is a concept and a case worth discussing, because so many of the difficult aspects of family relationships which harm the kids following divorce are exemplified in it so very clearly and miserably.

This case was decided by the California Court of Appeals, which reviewed it after a lower trial court decided against the child's mother. She had custody of the disputed child and refused access to her own parents. The grandparents had reared the child from his birth until the mother married, 3 years later. Until that time, the mother had lived in the Midwest and had little contact with her son. After her marriage, she and her new husband moved to the same California town where she grew up and where her parents lived with her son. Soon after that, she sought the return of her son. Her parents would not give up custody. In fact, alleging that the child had been abandoned by their daughter, they attempted to adopt the child.

The daughter sued for custody and won, but the court provided visitation rights to the grandparents. A year after that, the daughter and her husband sued to terminate the visitation rights of the grandparents, alleging that they interfered and undermined their own parenting of the child. The trial court judge ruled that it was in the child's best interests for him to be visited by his grandparents, but the daughter appealed that decision.

The California Court of Appeals upheld the trial court's decision. The majority opinion stated, "Grandparent visitation is beneficial for a child's development, allowing for the establishment and later maintenance of an important family relationship extending beyond childhood." The child's mother and stepfather apparently continued to disagree. They moved to another state, effectively depriving the grandparents from seeing the child. More significantly and ominously, they also deprived the child the opportunity to see his grandparents.

It does not take a psychiatrist to diagnose the degree of hostility inherent in this struggle. Fortunately for me, I was not involved in this dreadful case, but it is apparent from a distance that long-standing rage between the grandparents and their daughter obviously spilled over into the relationships with the child. Most likely, neither the mother nor the grandparents were actually angry at the child, but they might as well have been. They could not have led him into a more grief-filled arena had they consciously willed to destroy him.

When one examines this case, even from this brief outline, it is obvious that a lot of trouble between the principals must have flowed under the bridge long before the mother even became pregnant with the child in question. That trouble certainly seemed to cause considerable resentment in her parents. Also, the trouble probably created resentment in the daughter, or, conversely, the preceding bilateral resentment may have created trouble at home.

Who knows how much provocation and counter-provocation must have gone on in that terribly disturbed family? Who knows just exactly how it was carried on after the mother returned with her new husband and when she took the child from her unwilling parents? Was she a good mother? Were the grandparents good parent figures? Can one state definitely that one side was pure and that the other side was villainous? All that one can state definitely is that both sides continued fighting over the child, but it seems as if the fighting was really an extension of old fighting which existed before the mother even became pregnant.

Previous chapters have discussed rage as a strong motivating force creating dissension between divorcing parents and affecting their children badly. This case is a shining example of such feelings, and don't think for a moment that it is exceptional. The same feelings which can be seen so clearly here might be seen just a little more hazily in battles between parents themselves. They may not have gone on for the number of years that the problems existed in this family, but they may have the same effect. The children are used as levers against the opposing party. The appellate judge was right and so was the trial judge. Grandparents are beneficial for children. So are both parents. The same kinds of manipulations and deviousness exist in contests between parents as in this case between parent and grandparents.

Clearly in this case the mother sacrificed the welfare of her child by depriving him of a relationship which had been significant, even crucial, for him since birth. That's how mad she was at her parents. She will probably admit that anger even as she denies any anger at her child. It takes a lot of anger at one's parents to deprive them by sacrificing one's own child. Likewise, it takes a lot of anger at an ex-spouse to deprive him or her by sacrificing one's own child. That happens far more often. The child is hurt in both instances.

These questions are for all divorced or divorcing parents:

• How angry are you at your ex-spouse?

— Angry enough to deprive him/her of the children?
— So angry that you fail to realize that you're really depriving the children even more?
— Do you care about that? More than you care about being mad?

Visitation Battles Are Dumb

It there is no battle over custody itself, one cannot simply assume that there is no resentment and that the parents will cooperate in the rearing of their children. It may just mean that there was no custody battle. That is certainly a plus, but the behavior of the parents after the divorce must demonstrate the same good judgment. They must put aside their resentments and must encourage the children to see the other parent as much as possible. The number of horror stories and accusations on Monday mornings is great, and the problems afflicting the children who are put through battles about visitation are pitiable, just as in custody battles.

I often wonder about visitation problems when I hear about them from my patients or from people sent to me by their lawyers or the courts. Even more than custody battles, they seem to be so self-defeating. Let us take the example of a mother who has physical custody of the children. Let us assume (it takes very little effort to make this assumption) that she remains terribly angry at her ex-spouse. He is a fellow who, apparently suddenly, decided for reasons incomprehensible to her that he no longer wanted to stay married. Her hurt has never been healed, and her rage continues to boil. She tries hard, though, to be an exemplary mother to her children, a tough task these days because she has to work part-time to supplement her income. The ex-husband continues to pay child support and nominal spousal support, but this is simply not enough to carry her and the kids through the month. Do you know people like this? Are you one?

The father calls the house and asks to extend the visitation time for an extra night. Maybe there is a special occasion—a baseball game, or a party with his family, or something else which ought to be seen as beneficial for the kids. But the mother does not see it that way because she is too blinded by her rage at her ex-husband. As she sees it, the bastard is simply not entitled to more than the court authorized. We can easily recognize that she punishes the children even more than her ex-spouse by this type of decision. In fact, in my experience, it is not even hard to get the mother (or the father in other cases) to see that, after the fact, unfortunately. But even when these parents are in psychotherapy, their recognition of what they have done may not automatically cause them to change what they will do in future situations.

I have been a psychiatrist for nearly 30 years. By now I should know that reason and logic have very little, if anything, to do with many human decisions and actions. But when I am faced with these situations I still shake my head in wonder because I recognize that, by depriving the children of the visit with the father, the mother is also depriving herself of an extra day off. Self-defeat is an extra burden which does not have to be added to those already imposed by divorce. It is hard enough to be a single parent without depriving one's self of an opportunity for a little free time.

———— . ————

These questions are directed to all divorced or divorcing fathers:

• If you ask for extra time with your children, why are you doing that?

— Do you really have something special, a real treat to share with them?
— Are you just trying to gain more time with them?
— Is that so bad?
— Are you really mad at custodial Mama and trying to get her goat by dreaming up these supposed treats for the kids?

———— . ————

The following questions are for mothers who should think hard about the questions just put to fathers:

• How do you respond to these situations if you suspect foul play?
• Do you let yourself become the heavy by preventing the children from participating in treats, regardless of the motivations underlying those treats?
• Do you think that fighting about the situations will stop the foul play?

Martyrdom and Manipulation

Sometimes parents who have custody of their children glorify themselves by fantasied martyrdom. They become drudges in their own eyes as well as in the eyes of their beholders who may get tired of hearing their sob stories. Somehow, it is essential for these parents to see themselves as victimized in such a manner that they can never allow themselves to breathe freely. The idea is not allowed into their awareness that they might derive a little enjoyment from not having the children with them 24 hours a day every day. These parents, usually mothers, present themselves to the world in this way as another method to get back at their husbands. Of course, they reason, the world will come to see those men as fiends, dumping all these terrible responsibilities on them while they go ahead with their flings and their mistresses!

I have known custodial fathers to do the same thing as they ignore opportunities for fuller lives by leaving the children with sitters. Their slave-like devotion advertises to the world that their hated wives were obviously unfit to rear the children. The martyrdom they choose often sanctifies themselves in their own minds as they make these accusations. Mother or father, the ploy is a real bid for sympathy from a hard world. Sometimes it works, but more often than not it becomes tiresome to the listeners.

Just try to get some of these single parents to breathe a little easier. Many will absolutely refuse. Sometimes there are reasons for this behavior over and above the neurotic benefits of martyrdom. Sometimes this obvious self-punishment is based on guilt feelings. I have treated many harried and over-burdened (by choice) parents who felt many pangs of guilt over their own roles in the breakup of their marriages. Those guilt feelings are usually not recognized by the bearer because they are generally unconscious, but they are strong motivators nonetheless. When we feel guilty, we punish ourselves, usually more effectively than others can punish us. Choosing to be miserably overburdened is, believe me, quite self-punishing.

Do not allow yourself to be swayed by the guilt and the depressing aspects of this very common behavior. Always keep in mind that it is also very hostile behavior, since the thrust is against the opposing ex-spouse. It is a very hostile act to make that ex-spouse look dirty in the eyes of the world. It is even more hostile to the children to use them as pawns to make the ex-spouse look even dirtier!

The thrust goes the other way, too. Visiting parents also contribute to the mess at times. Many visiting parents actually become pests, calling their former homes far more frequently than they might and for reasons which seem to have no basis in real need. Many of these visiting parents use the opportunity to call, ostensibly to discuss the children, in unconscious attempts to maintain contact with the divorced spouse. It may be the visiting parent's way of clinging to a marriage which is long gone.

Another very common problem is posed by the manipulative, more overtly hostile visiting parent who sets out to disrupt the custodial parent's household. There may be many reasons underlying this disturbing behavior. Sometimes it is simply a manifestation of continued rage toward the custodial parent. The visiting parent, by frequent changes of plan and constant provoking of the custodial parent, may be attempting to weaken the resolve of the custodial parent enough to get him or her to agree to a change in custody. These visiting parents do not seem to consider that their provocations also affect the children. When custodial parents become anxious or angry, the children are likely to bear the brunt of their anxiety. That, in turn, may cause upsets in the children, which are then pounced on by the visiting parent and lawyer. They will then accuse the custodial parent of inability to control or otherwise handle the kids.

Nowhere in my experience are the manipulative talents of people as well demonstrated as in disputes following divorce. The children are generally the pawns here. Even when the attempt is made (as noted above) to get the custody, or the visitation frequency changed by wearing down the custodial parent, the underlying primary purpose may well be to get back at the custodial parent rather than to take care of the children. As with custody cases, attempts are often made to rationalize visitation conflicts by trying to point out that the fighters are really only interested in the best interests of the children. As in custody battles, the parents may not be able to recognize that their problems are actually destroying the best interests of the children. In many cases, the tornado still blows after divorce, and in its eye there is little ability to be objective and dispassionate.

We can catalogue more characteristic visitation problems, but if you are divorced and are either a custodial or visiting parent, you may know more examples than I do. The best visitations are those handled warmly and informally by both parents. I have seen many cases in which the parents, although they maintain the most hostile feelings toward each other, continue to set up the best possible situations for their children. I have seen very hurt and angry mothers welcoming their ex-husbands into their homes so that the children can be helped with homework, with crafts projects, or with anything else with which they both believe the father traditionally ought to involve himself. That may sound sexist on the surface. I do not intend it to be.

To prove that, let me share one case I treasure. In this family, the mother was the custodial parent. She was far more creatively handy with tools than the father, but she felt it necessary for her son to have the benefit of working with his father. The father panicked at the thought of having to teach his son how to do something which he never really learned well himself. The mother thereupon taught the father at times when he could join her at the neighborhood shop center. Then, feeling far more secure, the father proudly helped his son build his school project. I am not that naive that I am unaware of the expression of hostility on the mother's part by this maneuver. It came out loud and clear in my office as she chortled about her ineffective husband. She may have felt the need to reduce her ex-husband's status by demonstrating his ineffectiveness and comparing it with her own effectiveness, but the end result for the child was a constructive one. That end result made my interpretation to her of her unconscious hostility a little easier for her to bear and to integrate. After that, she was even able to recognize how her demeaning attitude contributed to the divorce itself.

———— · ————

The following questions are directed to all divorced parents who have custody of their children:

- How do you feel about the visiting parent visiting the children in your home? How does your new husband or wife feel about it?

  — If there is discomfort, are the children affected by it?
  — Is it possible for them not to be affected?
  — If visiting in your home is easy, are the children stimulated to hope even more for a reconciliation?
  — Do you want a reconciliation? Is that why the other parent is asked over to visit with the chidlren?

The Blocking Custodial Parent

Often, the Monday morning calls complain about blocks against the visiting parents set up by parents who have custody of the children. Why do the custodial parents block those visits? Why do many custodial parents take advantage of the slightest hint of a developing runny nose in the child to prevent a visit with a loving parent over a weekend? Why do many custodial parents overreact to late returns by the visiting parent, or to late pick-ups by them, or to dirty clothes, faces, or underwear? Why do they pounce on those opportunities to complain about the visiting parents and their unreliability? You answer these questions. You already know the answers.

At times, visiting parents may not actually care for the child to the excellent standards that I hope are characteristic of the custodial parent. Perhaps the visiting parents do not have the kind of homes to which they can take the children and in which they can provide them with the same physical comforts as they have in the custodial homes. Perhaps the visiting parent is a father who has had little experience in actually taking care of his children, but who sincerely wants to maintain the relationship with them. He will certainly have to learn fast.

———— · ————

In any event, the custodial parent must always remember that the visiting parent has one great advantage over the custodial parent. That advantage is that the visiting parent is actually with the child at that time, and the child needs that contact. The contact is worth the possibility of the sniffles turning into a cold (they probably would anyway, even if the child stayed in the custodial home that weekend), or a torn pair of blue jeans, or a dirty face, or a late return, or an undependable pick-up time.

———— · ————

I frequently hear of cases in which visitation is prevented by the custodial parent because the child has a party, a little league or soccer game, a piano lesson or recital, or who knows what on the Saturday afternoon in the middle of the time scheduled for the visiting parent. I hear stories about children calling their visiting parents and telling them that they cannot visit that weekend because of these kinds of events. This often makes the visiting parent angry, not at the child, of course, but at the custodial parent. That anger, matched against the anger of the custodial parent, leads to more fireworks. Monday morning again.

Why in the world does this situation have to block visitation? Why can't the visiting parent take the child to the party, to the game, to the lesson, or to the recital? These events provide terrific opportunities for the visiting parent to share the child's life and interests, and they also provide the visiting parent with some structure for the weekend. Participating in these activities is a good way to avoid being a Disneyland parent. Observing children in action with their peers offers visiting parents a lot to talk about with their children. So many visiting parents have told me that they frequently find themselves at wit's end trying to talk with their kids. Conversations with kids about what they do and what the parents see them do represent real quality time for them.

What prevents this simple, helpful maneuver? Sometimes the custodial parent uses the scheduled activity as an excuse to block the visit. On the other hand, I have also known situations in which the custodial parent has attempted to do just what I have described here. In some of those cases, the visiting parent has refused. Sometimes, the visiting parent is so angry at the custodial parent that he or she will not agree to any suggestion made by the custodial parent, even if it is obviously beneficial for the child and for the child's relationship with the visiting parent. The rage goes both ways, and the blocks thrown by both parents hurt the child.

———— · ————

The following questions are directed to all divorced parents who do not have custody of their children:

- How often, or how regularly, are you late returning the children after a visitation with them? When you are go-ing to be late, do you call?

  — What kind of reception do you get, and how do you deal with it?
  — If the reception is angry, do you make it worse by responding just as angrily?
  — Do you foist the responsibility onto the kids by mak-ing them call instead?

- Do you make the custodial parent into the heavy by forc-ing him/her to deny an extra treat which will keep the children out much later?

  — Does that make you feel good? (Honestly, now.)
  — What does that do to the children's relationship with the custodial parent?
  — How do you *really* feel about that?

The Potential New Spouse

A major problem affecting visitation is how a custodial parent feels when the visiting parent begins to develop a serious relationship with another potential mate. Visiting parents seem to do this much sooner than custodial parents. Perhaps the visiting parent may even move in with the potential mate, and the developing feelings within the custodial parent may erupt suddenly and explosively. There may also be a marked reaction on the part of the child. The child's reaction can be a response based on the custodial parent's response, or it can be the child's own response.

The response of the custodial parent needs little explanation here. We have discussed at length the long-held, simmering feelings of rage and hurt, and those feelings become emphasized when the ex-spouse joins someone else. It is hardest of all to recognize that the ex-spouse actually prefers someone else—that wound hurts most of all. Many custodial parents of both sexes become depressed at these times. Ordinarily they cannot reach the ex-spouses to hurt them directly. Even if they use the children as pawns against them or even if they can vent their spleens at them, the odds are that the ex-spouses will still take up with the new mates. Thus, the custodial parent's reaction usually becomes what psychiatrists call *impotent rage*. It has no power to change the situation which gave rise to it. But the feeling has to go somewhere, and impotent rage is the type people are most likely to turn inward against themselves, resulting in depression.

Custodial parents facing these situations will often work very hard to prevent the child from visiting with the other parent. They will complain long and loud over the immorality of the situation, just like the father I described in Chapter 2. They will also complain about many other things, sometimes stretching many points to do so. But the message is consistent. They want to withhold the visitations of their children. They are terribly threatened by the presence of the visiting parents' new, potential or actual spouses, and they do not want their own relationships with their children to be jeopardized by them. As if they could, if the custodial parents remained sensible and sensitive.

Smart custodial parents welcome the benefits provided by just-as-smart stepparents for their children. Custodial parents know that in many cases good stepparents provide the major stability in the visiting parents' households. After all, the visiting parent is just as upset over the breakup of his or her household as is the custodial parent, and he or she needs the emotional buffering provided by a new mate, just as does the custodial parent. Of course, getting the custodial parent to acknowledge that the new stepparent may really be smart, good, or even a worthwhile person in general may be a herculean effort. Often, good reports from the visiting children only serve to make wounds smart more. If the custodial parent finds somebody first, his or her resentment toward the ex-spouse *may* not be as great. But if the visiting parent finds someone first, we can usually expect some fireworks.

The remarks by the children may not be complimentary. The poor opinions expressed by the kids may make the custodial parent feel better, but the children's opinions need to be evaluated very carefully. Is the new stepparent (or potential stepparent) really not so good? Or are the children really only voicing the spoken or unspoken feelings of the custodial parent? They know that they must support that parent and agree with him or her. After all, who is more important in their lives? The children depend far more upon the custodial parent than on the visiting parent. Again, it might not be fair, but it's the case. Even in intact households, children generally depend more overtly on one parent than on the other, usually the mother but certainly not always.

Custodial parents need to be so very honest with themselves at this juncture in their lives. They must examine themselves and determine just how much (*not if*; it is always there) their rage has influenced their children's opinions, decisions, and feelings. They must recognize that it is in the direction of providing their kids with real quality time when they determine that the new stepparent might actually be helpful for them and for their relationship with the visiting parent. Do you recognize your own need to do this?

I hear many custodial parents describing their ex-spouses' new mates in the most insulting terms. Who knows, perhaps they may be right! Perhaps the ex-husband's new girlfriend is really just a slut, or the ex-wife's new boyfriend is really just a money-grubbing son-of-a-bitch. But we have learned that the perceptions and opinions of people who are being divorced, or who may have gone through the mill in their own divorces, may not be accurate. They simply have to be colored by their hurt and disappointment, and their own egos must be soothed at times by demeaning their ex-spouses' new mates.

The same mechanism is often apparent within the children. Their egos have also been bruised by their feelings of being rejected by the parent who departed from the household. The children may not be able to perceive the new potential stepparent with any degree of clarity because they see him or her as a rival for the visiting parent's affection. The children feel that they are getting little enough from that parent, and to share what little they get may be too much to expect from them. That must be understood by the visiting parent.

Often, visiting and custodial parents stress the idea that the children will have to accept the fact of the divorce and must also accept the fact that someone else is entering the picture. They are right, of course. Although we shall discuss in more detail in a later chapter what the children of divorce will have to do to adjust, we must recognize again that the children must acknowledge the finality of the break. In earlier chapters, we discussed that they generally do not and that they maintain fantasies of parental reconciliation for years or even for decades. Those fantasies and the insistent denial of recognizing that the parents will have other people in their lives will have to be dealt with. But they should not be dealt with by rubbing the children's noses in that denial or in an enforced recognition of the threatening new relationship. Children will respond better to a potential new stepparent, or to any new and important person in the real parent's life, if the real parent will bring in the new person slowly and carefully.

———— · ————

When the visiting parent has a new significant other, the visiting parent must take pains to spend considerable time alone with his or her children, perhaps even more than before. Doing so, and speaking about the new person generally at first, and only then more pointedly, will make the transition easier. The same goes for when the custodial parent develops other relationships. For both parents, it is crucial that both keep their mouths shut about the new turn of events for the other parent.

———— · ————

These questions are directed to all divorced parents:

• What would you like to do with your ex-spouse's new mate?
— Beat him/her up?
— Break up that relationship?
— Embrace her/him for assuming responsibility for your ex-spouse?

• How do you talk about the new mate to your children?
• Even if you speak favorably, what do you *really* feel, and what vibes come across?

The Homosexual Parent

The sexual revolution has affected us in many ways. For example, the new significant other may not be a person of the opposite sex. This is a complicating factor, but it need not and should not destroy the still-necessary relationship with the parent who comes out of the closet. The responses of the heterosexual parent (who is usually the custodial parent) to the turn of events are, for the most part, predictable. Ordinarily, they include an attempt to block the children's contact with the other parent. Usually the custodial parent will cite a belief that the visiting parent's homosexual relationship will cause homosexuality in the children as well as taint them morally.

Research has demonstrated that this is not necessarily the case, especially if the children are of school age or older.* The sexual preferences of children develop before they reach school age, and it is unlikely that they will change by virtue of visiting with a newly recognized homosexual parent and his or her new mate. The visiting parent obviously had homosexual tendencies if not overt activities before the divorce, and the young children had plenty of opportunity to pick up any identification in that area from him or her when the family still lived together. Furthermore, the causes for homosexuality are not known. The child's identification with conscious or unconscious tendencies within a parent may be important, but it is not likely to be the only factor. How many children of homosexual parents actually turn out to be homosexual? Nowhere near as many as you might think.

I recognize that I am asking a lot from parents throughout this book. It may be that the idea of allowing their children to visit freely with a homosexual parent may be more than some heterosexual custodial parents can bear. However, the best interests of the child benefit in many such cases. The homosexual parent can continue to provide considerable love and affection so necessary for the child. Believe it or not *(but believe it!),* the homosexual parent can also provide the child with a positive source for relating to that parent's sex. Many homosexual par-

---

* Green, Richard, "Sexual Identity of Thirty-Seven Children Raised by Homosexual or Transsexual Parents," *American Journal of Psychiatry*, vol. 135, no. 6, June, 1978, p. 692.

— 116 —

ents are even custodial parents, and their children have developed heterosexually.

———— · ————

The following questions are directed to all divorced or divorcing parents who are homosexual:

• Do you want your child or children to be homosexual or heterosexual?

    — If the child is of your sex?
    — If he or she is of the opposite sex?

• How do you think your ex-spouse believes that you want the children to turn out?
• If your ex-spouse believes that you want the children to become homosexual and you do not, how have you tried getting your message across?
• If your ex believes that you want the children to become heterosexual but that you are not able to steer them in that direction, how have you attempted to reassure him or her?
• Do you need reassurance yourself?

Neutral Ground

To return to more mundane problems of visitation, lateness in picking up and delivering children seems to be a thorn in the side of many custodial parents. If they cannot learn to shrug their shoulders over this admittedly annoying, perhaps even provocative, habit they should absent themselves from the home when the children are to be picked up or dropped off by the visiting parent. A sitter ought to be there instead, and then there will be little opportunity for crises to occur based on rising anger at the lateness of the pick-up or delivery times.

Often the children are picked up by the visiting parent at school or at a nursery school. These can be excellent neutral grounds when the relationship between estranged parents is such that they are bound to fight if they contact each other when the children are being transferred from one to the other. Nowadays, with so many mothers having to work, when they or fathers have custody of their children they must place them during the day in various care centers if they are not yet of school age. Grandparents are often marvelous sitters. Although they may fight for visitation more and more, they rarely want to rear grandchildren as they did their own children by caring for them day after day. Thus, the preschools or day care centers often provide the mainspring of the child's stability when the parents continue to fight over custody or visitation and when there may be frequent transfers between one parent and the other.

To use the analogy from *Beyond the Best Interests of the Child,* even if one or both parents might be good psychological parents, the day center often becomes the psychological home. The children are there during more waking hours—and more consistently—than in either parental home. I have interviewed a number of little children who did not know their home addresses but who knew the locations of their preschools!

Child care centers are becoming increasingly significant in U.S. life. The reasons are obvious when one considers the divorce rate and the economic crunch. The degree of their significance can be appreciated when one becomes aware that a number of large corporations are establishing these centers adjacent to their own facilities so that their employees can use those services. A survey recently released by the American Management Association reveals the opinion of a number of corporate executives that providing child care for employees is compatible with corporate self-interest. The survey demonstrated that 75 percent of nearly 300 companies concluded that the benefits

of providing child care outweighed the possible problems.*
The trend toward corporate establishment of child care centers
is a new one, and most of the firms surveyed had established
their centers within the past 5 years. It is, indeed, a hopeful and
a realistic trend.

———— . ————

To summarize, problems of visitation may mean that there
has not been a custody battle, and that is all to the good. On the
other hand, visitation problems can follow custody battles, and
battles over visitation or access mean the same things as custody
battles: that the parents continue to fight and that their fighting
adversely affects the children. Custodial parents and visiting
parents must both learn that their own times with the children,
and the times the children spend with the other parent, must
be quality time. It must be untainted by bad-mouthing or other
stresses applied to the children, who long for good, continued
relationships with the visiting parents. Both the custodial and
visiting parents must recognize the benefits of those relationships for the children and for themselves.

---

* Magid, Renee, "Child Care Initiatives for Working Parents: Why Employ-
ers Get Involved," *Los Angeles Times*, Feb. 12, 1984, part VI, p. 14.

CHAPTER 6

· · ·

More Problems of Visitation: The Biggies

Coinciding with the upswing in divorce and custody and visitation battles, the media has recently captured the public's attention by emphasizing two issues which have since become indelibly associated in the public's mind with the problems of custody and visitation. It is rare that the feature pages or even the news pages do not run stories on child kidnapping by a noncustodial parent or about the allegations of sexual abuse of a small child by a noncustodial parent. The epidemic of these particular problems is so widespread that they deserve some special coverage here.

Kidnapping by a Parent

Many cases involving supposed sexual abuse of the child by the noncustodial parent—in most cases the father and the small daughter—result in few actual convictions for criminal offenses. Most often, the allegations remain just charges, with little evidence available to prove any of them. In contrast, the kidnapping of a small child by the noncustodial parent is a real event which must have already happened for it to be reported. In fact, it happens a great deal. Estimates of more than 100,000 cases annually have been made, and the tragic impression is gained that most kidnappings result in the child staying with the kidnapping parent. More often than not the kidnapping parent has been able to avoid the law and the custodial parent.

New laws, some with teeth, may well change that outcome. Now, because of federal intervention and public outcry, most states will cooperate with the state in which the kidnapping occurred and will process warrants for the arrest of the kidnapping parent. Extradition to the other state may be performed or trial will take place in the kidnapping parent's own state. In any case, charges will be pressed and a trial set. The charge will be a felony, and the punishment may be severe. In the past, it was very difficult to get the courts in the kidnapping parent's state to observe the rules set down in the other state's divorce court orders. And that difficulty was encountered only after the child and the kidnapping parent had been found, itself a problematic task.

Now a network has been established so that the task of finding the child and the kidnapping parent might be made significantly easier. The almost uniform use of social security numbers aids this process. Now those records are available for study, and the sites of deductions or check cashing can be located. The military services are also cooperating in this effort. Retirement checks or other documents are also made available for tracing. Although they still resent having to do so (all law enforcement agencies probably despise marital conflicts more than any other situation in which they might have to intervene), the FBI now is empowered to track down parent kidnappers. The old federal kidnapping law had teeth, too, but when the kidnapper was the child's own parent the judgment that no actual crime had been committed was widespread.

The usual situation is that the noncustodial parent will take the child from a nursery school or from a sitter. Although there are no statistics to bear this out, apparently most parent kidnappings do not occur within the framework of a standard visitation session. Most often, the visiting parent returns the child from the visitation at the prescribed time. It is when the visiting parent does not have access to the child regularly that most of the kidnappings occur. That parent may come in from out of town strictly for the purpose of taking the child. Although nurseries and other child care centers are instructed to deny the child to anyone other than the familiarly known parent or an assigned substitute, a valid parent is a valid parent. If a long-desired parent comes to see the child, the child will respond with joy, excitement, and love, and few day care centers will deny the mutual wish of parent and child to be together.

——— . ———

The following questions are directed to all custodial parents:

- Do you think your ex-spouse will kidnap your child?
- Is your ex that impulsive?
- If you fear it, might you be stimulating it by, for example, overrestricting visitation?
- Are there basic, fundamental differences between you, such as religious or sexual, which might lead your ex-spouse to decide that the child must no longer live with you?
- Finally, do you think that you are thinking clearly enough about the situation to be a good predictor of your ex-spouse's behavior?

——— . ———

The Effects of Kidnapping

Kidnappings are terrible for the child, the custodial parent, and even for the kidnapping parent. In the several cases in which I have become involved, the trauma has been extensive. The children suffer, of course, during the initial phase of the kidnapping, and then they suffer again when they are returned to their custodial parent. The initial suffering is based on the anxiety of separation from the usual home setting and routine and from the custodial parent. The suffering on return has to do with many factors, not the least of which may be regret at having to leave the kidnapping parent whom the child also loves. The loyalty conflicts stimulated in the children of divorce are horrendous without kidnappings. What kidnappings do to those conflicts can only be imagined.

The anxiety and other associated symptoms of the distraught custodial parent need no explanation, but that the kidnapping parent also becomes quite anxious is often overlooked. Fugitives are always anxious, and even when there were few legal mechanisms to force the children back, the kidnapping parents always kept looking over their shoulders. What the anxiety of the kidnapping parent does to the child can also be predicted, but, after a time, when there is less likelihood of apprehension, the anxieties of both parent and child would tend to ease. However, in their review of the effects of parental kidnapping, Dr. Diane Schetky of Yale and Dr. Lee Haller of Washington, D.C., report that problems continue in the children.* As a single example, disturbances of identity can arise in kidnapped children because of the frequent name changes and location changes which may accompany the kidnap, especially when the kidnapping parent is running scared.

Perhaps you have heard of the "Stockholm syndrome," so called because in the 1950s an episode occurred in that Swedish

---

* Schetky, D. H., and Haller, L. H., "Parental Kidnapping," *Journal of the American Academy of Child Psychiatry*, vol. 22, p. 279, 1983.

city in which hostages were taken for political purposes. After their eventual release, it was discovered that they had begun to identify with the causes and the attitudes of their captors and to develop feelings of real personal closeness to them. This phenomenon was then studied intensively during and after the Viet Nam war, when captured U.S. prisoners sometimes became allied with their captors. Celebrated civilian cases have also occurred, such as that of Patty Hearst.

Anna Freud developed a theory more than 50 years ago which she called "identification with the aggressor." In this country, we say, "If you can't lick 'em, join 'em!" This is the basic mechanism of the Stockholm syndrome. There is a regression, a mechanism whereby the prisoners become childlike out of a sense of fear and of abject dependence on the captors. That regression to a childlike state allows the identification with formerly despised or ridiculed standards to become effective. It is sometimes a life-saving phenomenon. If the prisoners did not identify, they might well be killed.*

This is what happens to many of the children kidnapped by their noncustodial parents, but they ease into that pattern with less friction and with less coercion than prisoners of war or hostages. After all, they have long loved the kidnapping parent from afar and have hoped for his or her return. Thus, in a sense the children are primed to identify with the kidnapping parent and, after a while, to perceive themselves as naturally being where they are. Of course, now they will miss the other parent. That will create problems, too, but the new relationship with the kidnapping parent usually turns out to be a solid one. If they are returned home, when they speak lovingly of the kidnapping parent the custodial parent will ordinarily believe that the child has been brainwashed. In fact, the Stockholm syndrome is one of the mechanisms of so-called brainwashing.

I have seen depression develop in children on their return to the original custodial home after apprehension. They often

* Freud, Anna, *The Ego and The Mechanisms of Defense*, International Universities Press, New York, 1946.

worry about the kidnapping parent, especially if severe punishment might be forthcoming. They hear that parent vilified as a criminal, and this hurts even more because of the child's identification with that loved parent.

Some kidnapping parents are severely disturbed, and the custodial parents may have exceptional reason to be distraught. On occasion, the kidnapping parent has physically traumatized the child. Sometimes there are dire threats of violence or death, and sometimes those threats are carried out. Sometimes there is violence without threats, as in the recent famous case of the kidnapping father who set fire to his sleeping child's motel room in California. The boy received severe burns.

Fortunately, most kidnapping parents are not severely disturbed—at least not to the extent that they are overtly psychotic or that they will threaten the child. There is no question, however, about the presence of some degree of emotional disturbance within anyone who commits an act of such desperation and such self-centeredness. The kidnapping parent obviously has little regard for the law and, more important here, little realistic regard for the child. There may be healing after a time by virtue of the Stockholm syndrome, but the concept of plucking one's own child forcefully or deviously from the child's familiar territory forces us to consider the emotional state of the perpetrator.

Until proven otherwise, all kidnapping parents are dreadfully angry at the custodial parents. In my opinion, until proven to the contrary, that anger is out of control in kidnapping parents. The rage overcomes any good judgment. Although there may be rationalizations such as unwillingness to continue paying child support when there is little contact with the child, the anger goes far deeper than that.

I mentioned self-centeredness; how much more self-centered can a person be when that person defies the law and the welfare of the child he or she claims to love, to have that child for one's own? The motivation to have the child may not be for the child's sake as much as to agitate the custodial parent.

There is no better way to do that, but the price to be paid is paid mainly by the child.

Anxiety and depression, with symptoms extending from sleep disturbances to school problems, are seen in children who have been kidnapped by noncustodial parents. When the children are returned to their custodial parents, even if they are happy to be returned, they may develop considerable hostility toward those parents. After all, the children reason, how can I trust them if they allowed a kidnapping to happen?

Many such kidnappings have not been reported because of many personal reasons, and many which have been reported were never solved. Many which had been solved by finding the child did not result in the return of the child. Many cases in which the child was returned did not result in professionals studying the child and following up on the findings to determine a predictable pattern. Much of what we believe we know about this phenomenon is anecdotal.

However, now that the states are cooperating, as is the federal government, cases of child kidnapping by noncustodial parents should diminish. When they occur, kidnapping parents should be tracked down with greater efficiency and speed. That will be all to the good, eliminating much trauma in the children as well as in the parents. Media attention to these episodes has resulted in greater public awareness, and it is hoped that that awareness will lead to more studies of the effects on the children.

One San Francisco child psychiatrist, Dr. Lenore Terr, has intensively studied the effects of kidnapping on a group of children.* These children were not kidnapped by noncustodial parents, but by three young men who commandeered their Chowchilla, California, school bus at gunpoint. The children were severely traumatized by that episode, in which they were

---

* Terr, L. C., "Chowchilla Revisited: The Effects of Psychic Trauma Four Years After a School-Bus Kidnapping," *American Journal of Psychiatry,* vol. 140, p. 1543, 1983.

driven around for 11 hours in two blackened vans and then buried alive for 16 hours in a truck trailer. Although this might be a greater trauma than kidnapping by a noncustodial parent, Dr. Terr's findings are suggestive and helpful in determining what might happen to other kidnapped children. She found that every child exhibited definite indications of significant anxiety after the kidnapping. She also found that the previous adaptation of the children was very important in determining the level of symptom formation and actual emotional illness after rescue. If the children had adapted and adjusted well before the episode and if they demonstrated good community and family bonding, they did better. However, none escaped residual symptoms of disturbance.

According to her article, "Important new findings included pessimism about the future, belief in omens and prediction, memories of incorrect perceptions, thought suppression [of events related to the kidnapping], shame . . . [and] . . . fear of reexperiencing traumatic anxiety. . . ." Repetitive nightmares of the kidnapping were common 4 years later, including dreams of personal death. A number of troublesome major personality changes were noted in the children. Brief treatment administered for between 5 and 13 months after the episode did not prevent the development of symptoms and signs of emotional disturbance 4 years later.

Is it inane to stress here that kidnapping a child does not generally provide him or her with quality time? Perhaps, but experience continues to demonstrate that many parents still do not recognize that children can develop severe mental or emotional illnesses as children and that those processes will be lifelong burdens to bear. Kids just don't bounce. They are susceptible to anxiety and depression as children, and they suffer for longer times because they have longer to live. They need shelter, not trauma. That may be inane, but it needs repeating.

New studies at the Western Psychiatric Institute and Clinic of the University of Pittsburgh have revealed the extent of childhood depression. It is definitely not an uncommon disease. Furthermore, the Pittsburgh findings indicate that depression lasts far longer when it starts earlier in life. I do not want to be misunderstood here. Depression in children is not only due to kidnapping by a noncustodial parent. Fortunately, most cases do not have this type of episode in the background, but many have divorce and parental battles in the background. Whether or not those battles were the actual causes of the depressions in the children, it is evident that stability and continued productive relationships with both parents serve as positive factors which can only help children.

———— . ————

The following questions are directed to all separated or divorced parents:

• What effect do you think kidnapping would have on *your* child?

— If you were the kidnapper?
— If your ex-spouse were the kidnapper?

• If you have basic, unsolveable differences with your ex-spouse, how do you believe that taking the child from your ex will help?

Sexual Abuse of Children, Real and Alleged

Abusive relationships with one or both parents are obviously not productive for children. In 1983, estimates of reported cases throughout the United States resulted in a figure of close to a million. Dr. Selwyn Smith of the University of Ottawa has written several books about the problems of battered children in Canada. International borders do not stop epidemics. Sometimes the abuse is so severe that children die from it. In 1982, 51 children died from abuse in Pennsylvania alone. Reports estimate that as many as 5000 children die by their parents' hands each year in this country. The "battered child syndrome" was described originally in 1962, and the publicity it stimulated resulted in the U.S. Children's Bureau developing model legislation for reporting child abuse. By 1967, every state in the union had passed its own set of similar legislation.

Even with effective legislation and publicity, true figures are hard to come by. Massive campaigns have been mounted to stimulate reporting by parents, doctors, and hospitals when abuse is suspected, but many cases remain unreported. Many cases are suspected in which suspicion is not strong enough to make people report.

Sexual abuse of children is a major aspect of this problem. Although more than 80,000 cases are reported a year, the real number of incidents may be as much as ten times higher. Sexual abuse of children is a very common crime, and it results in considerable pain for the affected child. The wounds often last throughout life. Those wounds do not only affect the child's subsequent sexual development and activity; they also affect self-image and many other more general aspects of personality development.

The considerable publicity devoted to the sexual abuse of children has emphasized the information that most episodes are between children and people they know. Children are supposed to be taught to avoid overtures by seductive strangers, but those strangers still find ways to approach the children and sometimes continue with physical contact. In many cases, though, familiar people are the seducers. Siblings (brothers *and* sisters—despite popular mythology to the contrary, it is not uncommon for adolescent girls to stimulate their younger brothers and form long-lived sexual attachments) and other relatives are perhaps the most common offenders.

Elderly grandfathers have been unjustly maligned as dirty old men. There are, indeed, elderly perpetrators and offenders, but, fortunately, most grandfathers are not in that class.

Even more fortunately, neither are most fathers. However, as with parental kidnapping, an epidemic has broken out—an epidemic of accusations of sexual improprieties between fathers and even very young daughters. The accusations are usually made by the ex-wives, and they stimulate a large number of battles over visitation. The mother will want to eliminate all contact with the father. The father fights that, not only to prevent the destruction of his relationship with his daughter, but also to maintain his good name.

What about those accusations? Are they true for the most part? Or, as some observers feel, are they untrue for the most part? Are many of the accusations manipulative attempts by ex-wives to get back at their ex-husbands and prevent them from having any legitimate contact with their children?

Dr. Ben Bursten of the University of Tennessee has written effectively about child abuse and about studies made of parents who abuse their children. He concludes that it is not always easy to detect whether actual abuse has occurred, much less whether the parent has perpetrated it.*† Children, especially very young children, seldom talk about abuse. Their ages may be factors, or their conflicting feelings about the events. Besides, abuse itself may be difficult to define. Physical or overt sexual abuse may be clear enough, but sometimes accusations are made of abuse in the vaguest and most ill-defined terms. The term "abuse" itself has become a real attention grabber. It is now a buzz word, and its presence in an accusation regarding activities with children will automatically ring an alarm bell.

Abuse can be a specific medical issue. The presence of an abusing force can sometimes be diagnosed or at least strongly inferred by medical investigation. Pediatric or gynecologic examination can determine whether there may have been vaginal

---

* Bursten, B., *Beyond Psychiatric Expertise*, Charles C. Thomas, Springfield, Il., 1984.

† Bursten, B., "Detecting Child Abuse by Studying the Parents," submitted for publication in the *Bulletin of the American Academy of Psychiatry and the Law*, early 1985.

penetration in a young girl. The presence of bruises or other tell-tale signs may indicate forcefulness on the part of the pene-trator. Semen can be tested for chemically in the vagina. Rape has become a national concern, and even hospital emergency rooms are now stocked with "rape kits" to determine whether such an event took place.

Even if it is determined that the action took place, that determination does not answer the question of who did it. To muddy the waters even more, in many instances it is impossible to determine whether actual rape took place, especially if the victim is male. Perhaps there may be bruises about the genitals, attesting to forced handling. However, more often than not, in homosexual play with a male child there are few if any objective signs to indicate that sexual contact actually occurred. Tragi-cally, sometimes the only sign might be the presence of a vene-real disease in the youngster, usually arising a couple of weeks after the episode.

If fathers are the culprits, force is rarely an issue. There are probably no overt, objective signs of the contact, homosex-ual or heterosexual. Likewise, there are probably few if any hints provided by the victim that the contact actually took place. Older girls may eventually become sufficiently confused by the situation, and they may also be made more aware of their rights through general publicity about such events. If so, they may begin to talk with their friends, their teachers, or their coun-selors in other areas. Girl Scout leaders are frequent reporters. Young boys rarely talk at all about this, and neither do pre-school-age girls. If more than one child is simultaneously in-volved in the visitation with the offending parent, the child who is left alone might eventually comment about the action. This happened in a case in which I became involved. That was a rarer experience of a disturbed mother instituting mutual sex play with her 4-year-old son. The 7-year-old sister reported it to the custodial father.

If the situation is not divulged via the child reporting it to a neutral adult or by another sibling reporting it, the actual validity of the experience may be in question. By reporting, I mean that the incident is initially related by the child or by a direct observer. Reporting does not mean that the incident is suggested to the child-victim who then acquiesces to the suggestion and makes it his or her own.

Sometimes anxious parents will question their children excruciatingly about their contacts and activities with the visiting parent. Such agonizing questioning usually is a product of the custodial parent's hostility and insecurity. The child then becomes the conduit of all kinds of information about the hated ex-spouse, a role which is very destructive for the child. Sometimes the custodial parent becomes very involved in his or her own fantasies about the ex-spouse. In other cases, the custodial parent seethes with such continuing rage toward the visiting parent that she (usually she) develops the idea inside of herself that the visiting father is a sex pervert who is molesting their child. The mother then exaggerates the significance of a basically innocent report by the child. All sense of proportion is lost when obsessive rage runs the show.

I have also known of many cases, as have many law enforcement agencies, in which it was apparent that the mother was consciously lying, making up a story about the visiting father and foisting it onto the impressionable child. By such moves, the mother was really attempting to blackmail the visiting father or otherwise harass him and destroy his relationship with their child. When the relationship with a parent is destroyed, the effect on a child is terrible, but the mothers in those cases did not appear to think about that. They were usually too carried away by the force of their own rage toward their ex-spouses.

———— . ————

These questions are directed to all separated or divorced parents:

• Why do you believe that your child may have been sexually molested by your ex-spouse?

— Looking back, did the idea really start in *your* mind, or was it suggested by the child's behavior?
— Could it have been suggested by hearing stories about other parents and children?
— Is it *really* that he or she is just a no-good bastard/bitch and that you *know* he or she is likely to do it?

The Effects on the Children

When these dreadful scams are perpetrated, the children suffer many times over. Not only is the relationship with a loving parent threatened, but loyalty conflicts are heightened in those children who probably have already had loyalty conflicts stimulated within them by the previous actions of the custodial parent (and perhaps by the visiting parent as well). When pointed, accusatory questions are put to children by a grilling parent, causing children to wonder about their relationships with the visiting parent, other problems are created as well. The sexual acts about which they are questioned are, of course, forbidden and bad. When they have actually occurred, the results on the children are bad enough. If they have not occurred, and if the custodial parent is framing the visiting parent by using the child as a club over the head, the guilt and shame feelings created in the child because of supposed participation in those activities are heightened.

Loyalty tests are always terribly destructive to children. Kids should never be placed in the position of determining, much less announcing, if they love one or the other parent more. Certainly, they must never be placed in the position of choosing between them, and most certainly they are hurt terribly if they are placed in the position of having to accuse one or the other.

The guilt and shame over the participation in the actions is compounded in the child's mind if the offending parent gets into trouble because of the child's confession, which is really eventually seen by the child as an accusation. What do children think about themselves after having put the finger on a sexually offending parent? What do they think about themselves if they do not implicate their offending parent? Incest, of course, is a nearly universal prohibition, but data are developing which indicate that it is not as uncommon in our own culture as previously thought. Many sexual episodes are reported between parent and stepchild, and some between parent and biological child. But they do occur.

A controversy is raging now in contemporary psychoanalytic circles regarding Freud's doctrine that most reported instances of incest brought to light on the analytic couch are really fantasies of the patient who had actually wanted close, even sexual, contact with the parent of the opposite sex during childhood. Some observers now believe that the reports do not represent fantasies but actualities, and that is the source of the controversy. Whether or not that is so, some psychoanalysts continue to insist that the feelings developed in the child are all-important—even more important than the possibility of the reality of the charge.

Even more controversies can be expected regarding the significance of actual incest. For example, Dr. James Henderson of the University of Toronto has studied many families in which incest has occurred.* He concludes, in contrast to usual public and professional opinion, that incest is not always harmful. By no means does his conclusion suggest that it is good, and I am quite certain that he and I would agree that incest hardly

---

* Henderson, J., "Myths About Incest," *Canadian Journal of Psychiatry*, vol. 28, p. 34, 1983.

represents quality time. But Dr. Henderson's findings are significant in that follow-up studies indicate that disastrous psychological and sexual consequences may not be the rule in
these cases. Perhaps most significant is his observation that in
most of these affected families, the individuals who participate
in the incestuous relationships are disturbed to some extent
before the actual relationships develop. Furthermore, Dr. Henderson's findings point out that the effect of incest might not be
separable from the effects of many other family problems, including such factors as low family income, poor education, and
poor child-rearing practices.

I am certain that Dr. Henderson's findings, even multi-
plied by similar findings by many other workers, will not ease
the anxieties of parents whose children have been victimized in
real incestuous relationships. Although the results of incest
may not always be bad, enough cases have provided enough
emotional illness early or later in life to cause us to view the
situation with some alarm. The alarm felt by the nonincestuous
parent is critical in determining the emotional significance of
incest in a child's life. The development of problems in the
child probably depends more on the response of the nonincestuous parent, usually the mother, than on the sexual activity
itself.

Dr. Maria Sauzier, clinical director of the Family Crisis
Program at the New England Medical Center in Boston, examined more than 150 sexually abused children, each within 6
months of the most recently reported episode.* She reported
that the damaging emotional effects of sexual abuse are rarely
seen at the time of the trauma and that they may take a long
time to develop, if, indeed, they do develop. Preschool-age children, according to her findings, may develop serious deficits in
intellectual or even physical development, and they may also
display such rare traits as cruelty to animals and other children

---

* From "Mother Important in a Child's Reaction to Sex Abuse," *Clinical Psychiatry News,* vol. 12, no. 3, p. 6, March, 1984.

and inappropriate or provocative sexual behavior. Apparently seconding Dr. Henderson's findings, she also noted that most pathology resulted from sexual abuse by a mother's boyfriend, a stepfather, or a casual parental figure. Less psychological damage resulted from actual paternal incest.

Furthermore, Dr. Sauzier emphasized that the role of the mother is critical. The mother has the capacity to minimize the trauma or maximize it by making the child feel unprotected and condemned. The nonincestuous parent is the adult needed most by the child, since feelings of conflict about the sexual relationship can probably be elicited in most victims. The conflicted feelings of the developing child can cause the child to form personality problems which may be troublesome in later years, sometimes creating sexual and other problems during adulthood. Paradoxically, it might be easier to relieve the adult patient's guilt feelings if it is determined that a sexual contact actually did take place between child and parent. After all, it will be assumed that the child was the innocent victim, even though the episode may have led to some gratification within the child. But that feeling of gratification, even in a preschool-age child, is the real culprit. Young children may not have sexual feelings in the way that adults do, but they have comparable feelings often triggered by stimulation of their genitals. Most parents have seen their small children masturbate. The children do that because it feels good, and it is gratifying.

On the analyst's couch, the adult patients eventually learn that their guilt stems from the fact that, in part, they really enjoyed the contact with the parent—a feeling even more prohibited and bad than the contact itself! If there was no real contact, then the childhood wishes for contact will have to be elicited, and the guilt and shame resulting from those wishes might be harder to treat than the problems of actual contact. There is no victimization in those cases to soften the feelings.

The following questions are directed to all separated or divorced parents:

• As a child, were you ever approached sexually by an adult?

— Of the same sex?
— Of the opposite sex?
— Of your own family?

• Did the approach result in actual sex play or contact? Was it repeated? Was it discovered?
• Looking back, always trying to be as honest as possible, how would you have liked the episode treated then? Did you want the relationship terminated?

— The total relationship?
— Just the sexual part?
— Either or neither? (Be honest, now.)

Is It True or Not?

When custodial parents grill their kids about possible sexual contacts with the visiting parents, they are instilling more problems into the children than can be described here. All parents must be aware that sexual molestation does occur and that it may be occurring more than is currently realized. Suspicion of possible sexual molestation may develop when the child begins to manifest some of the signs noted by Dr. Sauzier. Perhaps there is more masturbation activity or a sudden increase in sexual curiosity or preoccupation. Perhaps there are even bruises around the genitals. But the visiting parent is not the only source for molestation of the child, and accusations must be made very carefully, no matter how angry the custodial parent is at the visiting parent. In any case, hammering at the child is a better way to make the child sick than it is to elicit information.

Proving the charge is always a problem. In practically every instance, the accusation will be denied. Often polygraphy is resorted to, a dubious and confusing method of truth determination at best. Sometimes psychiatrists or psychologists are asked to examine suspects to determine if they have the type of personality which might predispose them to such activities. This is stuff and nonsense. It represents only the most superficial and circumstantial character evidence, which in many instances is correctly determined by judges to have no validity. I have known of many cases in which the accused is felt to be guilty by the examiners because he or she sticks to the denial in the face of repeated questioning. The examiners then have stated that the suspect shows no insight into the fact that he or she performed the action!

Police investigations are geared to the determination of truth. Those of mental health experts are not. Psychiatrists are far better able to help in a different area. Incest represents a family problem when it actually occurs, and that family problem must be treated. If it does not really occur but the charge is made, that, too, represents a real family problem, and that must be treated as well.

Treatment of the Abuse Complex

Widespread, creative, and quite remarkable research has been very productive in enlarging our knowledge about incest, its patterns, its occurrences, and its sources. Most important, it has led to greater insights into its treatability. You may be surprised to learn, for example, that in many cases of father-daughter incest, the mother is aware of it long before it is otherwise discovered. Often, because of tensions which have long existed within the family, the mothers might actually push their daughters into these relationships with their fathers. Most instances have occurred in families within which the sexual relationship between father and mother has long since deteriorated. The sexual relationship is a good barometer of the other aspects of the mother-father relationship, and it can easily be determined that the bloom had long faded from those as well.

What should happen in these cases of incest, whether in an intact or a divorced family? Research has demonstrated that family therapy is the preferred method of involvement. Jailing the offender, usually the father, does no good in most cases. Most law enforcement agencies are aware that many mothers generally stick with their husbands, even after accusing them, often visiting regularly in prison and waiting impatiently for their releases in order to reunite. If they and the children are ordered to live apart from the husbands, the mothers often cheat. They visit in the husband's new home or even encourage the husband to return to the old household despite the court order.

It does not take a psychiatrist to wonder about the feelings of that species of mother toward the daughter with whom the father may have had sexual relations. Is the daughter seen solely as an innocent victim in those cases? Probably not. More than likely the daughter will be resented as a rival, even if the mother denies this and even if it can be demonstrated that she played a significant role in setting up the situation. Incest destroys many aspects of family relationships, not only those between offender and victim. Everybody is a victim. If the child is already a child of divorce, with an already traumatized family, the problem is made worse from the outset. The baseline is already too far out.

In these cases, should there be no relationship at all with the supposedly offending parent? In most instances, destroying that relationship prevents healing of the problem which had developed or preexisted in the relationship. The child must relearn to trust the parent who also must learn to trust himself or herself. The guilt must be properly directed, not shared with the child, and that is best done between the offending parent and the child. The enormous problems of self-image which would ordinarily develop following sexual relations with one's own parent can be softened, if not eliminated. The other parent, too, needs much help in dealing with this problem. In cases of father-daughter sexual abuse, the mother's maintaining of the rage she might feel toward the offending father will tend to cause identification with that rage in the daughter. The daughter's rage and fears will be directed not only toward the father, but toward most men she meets in her life. Without help for all concerned, a difficult life can be expected for her!

Enlightened courts have developed programs for family treatment of incest or of incest which has been charged and not disproved. In those jurisdictions, visitation with the offending parent continues, but always in the presence of a third party. Sometimes the third party is the family therapist. Sometimes it is a neutral person. The offending parent is not jailed. Incarceration prevents him or her from working, from paying child or family support, and from paying for the needed therapy. The courts have begun to recognize that most incestuous fathers are not just garden-variety pedophiles who might prey on random or otherwise-selected children. They have learned that these particular fathers are not general social menaces and that specific psychodynamics are generally present which lead them to develop sexual relations with their own children. The courts have also learned that without family intervention, problems are created for the future.

———— · ————

Throughout this book, I have emphasized the need for honesty and self-examination for all parents, together or divorced. So many avenues for revenge against a rejecting ex-spouse are open to vindictive individuals. It is easy to get another person in trouble. Charging an ex-husband or an ex-wife with sexual molestation of children is a terrific way. It is guaranteed.

There is no challenge in venting your spleen against a hated someone. The challenge is in controlling your feelings, and to do that effectively you must acknowledge to yourself what you are feeling. If you let yourself be carried away by troublesome feelings, your children will be hurt. Your children need protection against such heinous crimes as kidnapping and sexual molestation. If those situations occur, they must be attacked instantly, but we can all be thankful that these types of problems do not affect most of us.

Do not invite problems for your children by becoming preoccupied with fears that terrible crimes will be perpetrated by your ex-spouse. Divorcing parents must not fantasize horrid situations as drains for their hostility toward those same ex-spouses. Instead, they must insist that their children receive the benefits from free and open contacts with their visiting parents. Fearsome ideas implanted into children by manipulative parents destroy families. When families are destroyed, who provides quality time?

CHAPTER 7

— · · · —

Fathers—or Maybe Fathers and Mothers

Most men probably would not agree with me that the women's movement has benefitted them. Perhaps most divorced men would think me absolutely crazy or at least a traitor to my sex for even considering such an idea. But feminism has given birth to the very significant new trend of single fathers assuming the custody of their children.

The role of women through the years has been a thankless one in many respects, maybe even in most respects. Earlier, I reviewed the legal aspects of the rights of women as wives and mothers. To summarize, they had just about none until the early years of this century. Until then, lawyers studied for their profession by reading the texts of the great English jurist, Sir William Blackstone. He wrote, "The very being or existence of the woman is suspended during the marriage, or at least is incorporated and consolidated into that of the husband: under whose wing, protection and cover, she performs everything. . . ." Blackstone even went further, telling us that, "The courts of law will . . . permit a husband to restrain a wife of her liberty, in case of any gross misbehaviour. . . ."*

Has the worm turned? Perhaps to a degree, but women involved in the crusade tell us that some of the supposed gains are more apparent than real. Perhaps there are a few more female executives in corporations, and more are definitely entering the professions. But many women are wondering if these gains are worth the struggle. A number of women are loath to give up their previous domestic existences. They are seen as traitors by their more aggressive sisters who demean their lives and their family-centered goals. The mothers who insist on domestic existences are made to feel guilty and ashamed because of their "unworthy" stance. Those feelings cannot help but affect the children in those families.

Women have no need to feel guilty or ashamed about their preferred roles as mothers and wives, if those are their genuinely preferred roles. Likewise, they have no need to feel guilty if they choose careers in life which take them away from those classic roles. Many career women have been excellent mothers as well. The successful ones, like successful career fathers, know how to balance the demands made on them by home and the outside.

———— · ————

The following questions are directed to all separated or divorced mothers:

• Have you ever participated in feminist groups or in consciousness-raising sessions?

— If so, have you been stimulated to believe that careers have greater personal value than domesticity?

* "Experts, Custody Disputes and Legal Fantasies," *The Psychiatric Hospital,* vol. 14, p. 140, 1983.

— In contrast, have you determined that a domestic existence is more personally valuable to you?
— Have you resolved your doubts about your goals and your identity as a woman?
— Regardless of your direction, do you take pride in your chosen sexual role?
— What do your kids feel about all this?
— Do your sons feel differently from your daughters? Should they?

The Changing Roles of Fathers

In the same manner that women had been relegated to servant status, fathers had been relegated to a role just as demeaning in its own way. Fathers had been the breadwinners of the family, the sources of law governing all of its members, and, by and large, the individual with whom there was generally only a rather peripheral and often quite structured relationship. Mother was, of course, the fountainhead of warmth and comfort for the children. Fathers may have taken pride in their families, but they always seemed to give the kids back to Mama whenever they were troublesome or, as infants, wet. When they required discipline, "good old Dad" was there with a strap or a strong hand, but it was not considered good form for the masculine heads of families to dispense affection. If the children were boys, the father would take special pains to teach them the manly arts of self-defense, sawing, hammering, and all the other supposedly masculine aspects of life. If he did not become tongue-tied, he might even teach his sons the facts of life.

As comparatively little as they had to do with their sons, classic fathers had even less to do with their daughters. It was fine to kiss daughters (although *never* their sons), and the fathers sometimes suffered nobly through the dance recitals or piano recitals. Probably more often they did not go at all, leaving the cultural developments to their wives. Those were supposedly the refined, feminine virtues.

These clichés do not represent only the fictional fathers we have all read about in old novels or even in comic strips. These stereotypes were—and are—awfully real. They continue to provide a framework for a lot of heartache. The longings of children of both sexes for closer relationships with their fathers were not recognized until the first psychoanalytic researchers began to listen to their patients in the early years of this century. Even despite that recognition, fathers have generally continued to take a back seat as significant parents. Mothers and fathers have both been wrong in positioning them there.

Fathers may have placed themselves in that position, often distancing themselves from the emotional side of their relationships with their kids. Nevertheless, their kids continued to long for more closeness with them. Even boys who longed for their dads as kids and who grew up to be fathers continued the distancing they learned at their own fathers' knees. They identified with the stereotyped male role in the family. Whether that role model was an older Archie Bunker or Oliver Wendell Holmes's *Autocrat of the Breakfast Table,* father learned to see himself in ways we can now recognize as most peculiar.

Over the last 50 or so years, the images of fatherhood in our culture have changed to a remarkable degree. Possibly the most radical of those changes have occurred within the past 15 years, concurrent with the developing feminist revolution. But the roles assumed by both parents began to change considerably beginning with the great depression of the 1930s, when fathers in so many families toppled from their thrones because they could no longer provide. The depression was followed by World War II, when the men went away and the women went to work.

The children of the depression and of the war saw something different in their own families than their own parents had seen when they were growing up. Those children frequently became confused over parental roles as well as confused over the ways their parents related to each other. Who was the real boss in those families? Often, the father continued to be considered the head of the household, but the mother made all the decisions, including financial ones. When the money began to be controlled by feminine hands, real changes occurred, and these further affected relationships with the children.

The children in these families grew up and reared children of their own. They blurred the old, strict demarcation between the sexes and between the way each sex related with the children. I do not defend the ancient, stereotyped roles— they were poor at best, and they created untold generations of sterile relationships between fathers and children. But clear and well-defined roles were present to provide models. They were definite roles, even though poor ones, and they did not stimulate confusion in the children. However, the role models which followed these changes were often vague and ambiguous for both male and female. Confused parents rear confused children who, themselves, rear confused children of their own.

When women became stronger in families, men *sometimes* became weaker. It was certainly not necessary for men to perceive themselves as weaker if their wives worked, even if their wives made more money than they did or even if the wives made all the money in the family. If the men saw themselves as weaker, it was because they suffered from that longstanding false premise that they had to be the breadwinners and the lords and masters of their castles. In smart families, the parents learned to share the responsibilities of earning the living, and when that was shared it became necessary to share the responsibility of rearing the children as well. No self-respecting woman should have to work all day and come home to have to do *all* the cleaning, washing, cooking and child care, but will a self-respecting man work all day and come home to do *his* share of those chores which his own father might have seen as below his station? He had better! The great thing is that these tasks are simply becoming part and parcel of their lives, and they are definitely not below their stations! The old, outmoded expectations are definitely changing—perhaps not as rapidly as they should, but at least in the right direction.

———— · ————

These questions are directed to all separated or divorced fathers:

• How were you reared? Was one parent the boss in your family as you were growing up?
• Was there affection?

— Between your parents?
— Between them and you?
— Between your father and you?

• Would you have liked the relationships changed?
• Are you unwittingly repeating them with your own children?

Fathers and Children

Thankfully, many husbands have learned to be fathers in the real sense of the term. Their families have benefitted remarkably from that knowledge, and the fathers themselves have also benefitted from participating where they had not before. Until recent years, most studies of fathers in families have focused on the effects of absent fathers on the abandoned or rejected children. With the advent of feminist awareness and the increasing independence of women, researchers have turned their attention to the effects of fathers who are present and active in families. The results of these studies are overwhelming and consistent.* The importance of fathers has been grossly undervalued in the past. Only now is the father being

* Price-Bonham, S., "Bibliography of Literature Related to the Role of Fathers," *Family Coordinator,* vol. 25, p. 489, 1976.

recognized as the significant personage he is to his children of both sexes and of all ages.

Father-child interaction plays a very significant role in facilitating child development. Most people have no problem recognizing that fathers of older children may become quite close to the kids, especially adolescent children, not only as disciplinarians but also as companions. Even today, however, many people do not recognize that fathers can be just as close as mothers to very young children and infants, and can influence those children equally.

Fathers can nurture their children. They can love them, clothe them, feed them, change them, counsel and comfort them, and do everything for them that mothers can do, with the sole exception of breast feeding. Moreover, they can do all those things—and more—well and effectively, without any sense that these jobs render them less masculine. Fathers can do these things if they have custody of their kids, and they can do them if they are visiting parents. They no longer have to be Disneyland parents, even to very young children. "Mothering" is now a term which has nothing to do with the sex of the person who provides that care. The same goes for fathering, I suppose, although we never seem to see that term used very much. (I dislike the term "parenting"; it seems a rather cold, clinical, and detached description of what should be a loving relationship.)

Family law specialists and judges are beginning to award custody of even young children and infants to fathers because they recognize the fact that fathers can now be good mothers, but one factor must be recognized when a decision is made to grant custody to a father—the motivation of the father to assume the custodial role. It is easy to say, "I really want that kid!" Either parent can say that and do battle over the concept. But the predivorce relationships within the family must be determined. Those are often the best clues to the presence of true motivation. A father *can* nurture his children, but the judge must always ask the question, "*Has* he?"

Now, of course, everybody works, especially if they are divorced. It is a rare divorced woman who is supported by alimony or other forms of spousal support to the extent that she does not have to seek employment. Working women are the product of the economic and feminist revolutions. Those social movements have created an atmosphere in which the idea of fathers assuming custody of their children has become common and acceptable. Those fathers who want custody, no matter how angry they may be at their "libber" wives, ought to be grateful. Without the restructuring of our lives created by the women's movement, the kids would have continued to go to their mothers, just as they had since the turn of our century. It is the women who have overturned the tender years doctrine!

———— . ————

The following questions are directed to all separated or divorced fathers:

• How skillful are you?

— At changing diapers?
— At bottle-feeding or spoon-feeding babies?
— At bathing babies?
— At holding heads over toilet bowls?

• If you are not skillful at these things, why not?
• What are your real feelings about doing these things?
• What would your feelings have been toward your own father if he had done them? Did he? If not, why not?

Parents Who Feel Guilty

Fathers in families where both parents worked have backgrounds in child care. This is a new role for many men, and they find it a congenial one in many respects. Child rearing is congenial, even though it is often a severe pain in many or all portions of the anatomy. The responsibilities are enormous, and the lack of rest or time for one's self often causes parents of either sex to become enormously frustrated. I have heard fathers tell me that they find it relatively easy to get sitters for their children so that they can go out several nights during the week and relieve the pressure they feel. I have also heard mothers tell me that they do not find it as easy to hire sitters, not because they lack the money to do so but because they feel that they ought not leave the children. Stereotypes die hard.

Mothers somehow are more prone to feel guilty about their children and their rearing of them. When they have to go to work to help support them, there are often many episodes of tears on both sides. I hear working mothers tell me, "My kids spend more time with others than they do with me. We have so little time together." I have never heard a similar complaint from a single father. Most single fathers, in fact, appear to take considerable pride in the time that they do spend with their children. That time may or may not be quality time, and the fathers may also indulge themselves with more opportunities to get away from the kids at night than they really need. However, expressions of guilt from them are rare enough that I have never heard them. The mothers seem to have a monopoly on those feelings, but they don't have to feel them. Unlike working mothers, working fathers have the advantage of an ancient cultural expectation that they will work and support their families. That has not been the cultural expectation for mothers. But mothers will, increasingly, get used to the idea that they have to share their children with day care centers, nursery schools, or other resources for the care of their children. Their guilt feelings over having to do that will become as rare as those of today's single fathers. The mothers may even begin to feel better about hiring sitters so that they can get out and share a little more adult company.

Today's single mothers must adapt to necessities better. They must dispense with their guilt feelings, not only for their own sakes but for the sake of the children as well. Kids suffer when they grow up with guilt-ridden parents, and they often make other people suffer too. Sometimes parents deal with their own feelings of guilt by indulging the children, a practice which results in spoiled kids who unrealistically learn to expect that they are entitled to that treatment. My experience with single mothers leads me to believe that their best approach to guilt relief is to know that they are leaving their children in the best possible hands, and they should investigate the schools or the day care centers thoroughly. Compare one with the other. Talk with other mothers. Get references.

When you are with your children, *don't cry over your having to work.* Take pride in your ability to work and in your ability to support the family. That will help create a positive and constructive role model for children of both sexes. *Don't cry with them over your inability to spend more time with them,* even if the children themselves bring up the idea. Children have a remarkably well-developed capacity to stimulate guilt in parents, a capacity advanced far beyond their years. Single parents bring enough guilt into their relationships with their children without the children stimulating more. Instead of playing into the guilt-promoting wiles of the children or giving in to your own guilt feelings, use the time with them to work with them. Praise them for what they have done in school or in the nursery. Let them know about your life and your activities. Use the time to love the hell out of them.

Come to think of it, I have no better advice for single fathers, either.

———— · ————

These questions are for all separated or divorced mothers who have custody of their children:

• How susceptible are you to guilt feelings stimulated by your children?

— How good were you at that game as a child?
— Did both of your parents work?
— If so, how did *they* feel about that?
— What have you learned from them and from your own childhood?

In Praise of Flexible Households

Single parents of both sexes must make many adjustments to their new roles. Some of the most mundane events are changed by the new status. One of the most basic, for example, is the shift in dinner times. In the classic intact family, the father comes home from work, and almost without delay there is dinner, hot and steaming on the table. Working single parents cannot do that. Microwave ovens may help, but not as much as attitude adjustments. Meal planning must now take work into consideration, and the supposed needs of the children for hot meals three times a day might go by the boards at times. More guilty breast beating? Not necessarily. The kids won't suffer too much.

Single fathers may not have been the cooks in their married households. As an art, fine cookery is difficult to achieve, but as a skill, it can be learned without too much trouble. Besides, haute cuisine is not the rule on most tables, even in the most affluent and intact households. Meals shared between children and parents represent quality time if there is love, even if the food is cold. Sandwiches filled with good stuff can be just as nourishing as the full course meal. A treat, in fact, like a good dessert brought home, can make the night for everybody.

Different types of meals represent a change in lifestyle. A different lifestyle is the inevitable result of divorce and single parenthood. The fact that a lifestyle is different does not mean that it is bad. I have heard many grandparents cluck-cluck over the manner in which their grandchildren were being reared by their single parents, especially by their single fathers. Careful questioning usually revealed that the kids were not really troubled over and above what would be expected. They were usually found to be doing well and adjusting well. Their school and other activities continued unaffected. These are excellent barometers indicating how children are adjusting. Before people complain about how children are doing in their new environments, they should determine how the kids are achieving expected goals in academic, athletic, and social interaction.

Structure is often the most sacrificed commodity in single-parent households. The seeming lack of organization and routine is probably the most disturbing facet of the new household to observers who are used to more structure in their own lives. But the fact that they do not perceive structure does not mean that it does not exist. For instance, organization might appear lacking when the children assume more responsibility for household and family chores. Households can be more flexible and still be organized.

Children may have to make their own lunches — and maybe father's or mother's lunch as well. Lunches can even be made together. Grocery shopping becomes a family excursion. A little relaxed or fun time during that process makes it into less of a chore and more of an outing. The shopping can still get done, even with the accompaniment of a few laughs. All these shared activities can be real quality time during which both parents and children learn the fine art of give and take.

———— · ————

The following questions are for all separated or divorced parents who have custody of their children:

• How bothered are you by the comparative lack of structure in your household?

— In contrast, is your household quite structured?
— If your household is structured, how do you make it possible?

— If the household is unstructured, are your thoughts often drawn to fantasies of intact family life? How do they make you feel?

— Do you use opportunities for your children to assume increased responsibilities? Are you proud of using those opportunities?

— In contrast, are you guilt-ridden? Do you work harder to do more for them because, after all, they are living in a single-parent household?

Children Need Their Fathers

Judges have learned that single fathers can be flexible, can learn to cook, can nurture their children, and can, all in all, serve as effective single parents — just as single mothers can. Moreover, they have learned from data, not just from prejudice. Just as a single example, in the recent followup to her original studies, Dr. Judith Wallerstein has demonstrated that the female adolescent children of divorce do better when they have a close relationship to the father, whether or not the father has actual custody. According to her data, the female children develop more wholesome and fulfilled concepts about their own sexuality and femininity by virtue of having the father around. The presence of fathers is urgent for developing girls.

Dr. Laurence Loeb, a New York psychiatrist, has also called attention to the special needs of adolescent children.* He has written that, at that stage of growth, the presence of fathers may be more essential than at earlier stages and that the pres-

---

* Loeb, L., "Fathers and Sons: Some Effects of Prolonged Custody Litigation," submitted for publication to the *Bulletin of the American Academy of Psychiatry and the Law,* probably to appear in early 1985.

ence of fathers is critical for both male and female adolescence. Male teenagers look to their fathers for external control and discipline in the face of unbounded, often troublesome, impulses. The fathers are necessary role models here. Of course, mothers are also able to exert control over these tendencies, but many do not yet feel sufficiently secure in that role. They will, with practice.

Adolescent girls use their fathers as their initial sex objects, that is, they learn about men via their fathers, and they practice their emerging identities and roles with them. Referring to prolonged child custody or visitation litigation, Loeb has pointed out that one outcome is, ". . . the tragedy of the loss of the father to the adolescent-to-be as well as of the emotional loss of the child to the parent. . . ."

Along those same lines, Dr. John Jacobs, at the Albert Einstein College of Medicine in New York City, has studied many divorced and divorcing fathers.* He has reported on his treatment of numerous crises in these men based on their feelings of loss of the children and loss of their status as fathers. In contrast to considerable public expectation, they can bruise just as easily as mothers. Moreover, they can demonstrate the same sensitivities and needs for contact with their children. This is emphasized here, not out of any sympathy for the fathers' needs since the children's needs are what count in this book, but, rather, to demonstrate that the presence of those needs in men indicate that they have the capacity for closeness to their children, just as the mothers do. If sensitive single fathers assume their custody, children of both sexes and all ages can do well. Judges are finding that out and are acting on that knowledge.

---

* Jacobs, J. W., "Treatment of Divorcing Fathers: Social and Psychotherapeutic Considerations," *American Journal of Psychiatry*, vol. 140, p. 1294, 1983.

The following questions are directed to all separated or divorced fathers:

- What do you do with your daughters that is comparable to playing ball with your sons?
- If the daughters are preadolescent or adolescent, how do you respond when they talk about boys?
  — Do they talk about this or, for that matter, about anything, with you?
  — If not, why not?
  — Despite your verbal assurances to them, what attitudes are you somehow expressing which may cause them to cut off their impulse to talk with your?
  — Even if you don't recognize such an attitude, are you willing to consider that such vibes are being sent out? What are you going to do about that?

Help from Support Groups

My experience with single fathers has led me to perceive that they suffer basically the same difficulties that single mothers do. It is terribly difficult to rear children without a second parent of either sex. It is terribly difficult to rear children without support and encouragement from someone close. Single mothers get terribly frustrated. So do single fathers. So do the children.

Frustration is often somewhat relieved by finding that it is shared and that the suffering party is not alone in the world. Many single fathers have learned that support groups have developed to provide help for them, just like the groups which had developed for divorced mothers over the years. However, some groups have been formed for noncustodial fathers that, under the guise of teaching the disenfranchised fathers about their rights, stimulate the reopening of long-lost custody battles. These will do nothing but aggravate the situation more to the vast detriment of the children.

Support groups can help single parents of both sexes a great deal as long as they do not stimulate more conflict. I encourage all divorced parents to join several groups, at least one of which should be a group which has both mothers and fathers in it. I know that some of those groups only serve to introduce divorced parents to each other to get them to date each other, but it is nonetheless necessary to communicate openly with parents of the opposite sex. An enormous amount can be learned by doing that, and, after all, you don't have to date anyone if you don't want to.

Fathers and Mothers and Birds and Bees

Even with the aid of a support group, there is one particular area in which single parents may feel a considerable sense of inability to perform if they have custody of children of the opposite sex. I have saved this until the end of this chapter, but definitely not to leave you laughing. The inability to discuss sex with a child of the opposite sex is a very serious problem adversely affecting relationships between parents and children. I have listened to single mothers plead with me to serve as a surrogate father so that I could discuss the birds and the bees with their sons. Likewise, I have heard single fathers tell me that they find it almost impossible to discuss sex with their daughters, even though they are aware that the girls will soon be approaching their menarche and will begin having menstrual periods.

In this supposedly liberated age, it seems paradoxical that many adults will not allow themselves to teach their children about sex. Often single parents expect their children to recognize and even understand sexual behavior which might be going on between the single parent and a new companion, often in the same household with the children. But, to talk about this and to teach children about the good feelings that are stimulated between the sexes, that indicate growing up and require increasing responsibility and control, appears to be beyond so very many parents, whether married or divorced. If parents fight for custody of their children, they fight for the responsibility to rear them, and that includes teaching the children about sex, regardless of whether the children are of the same or different sex as the single parent. School sex education courses are just not enough.

I have spoken with many single parents about their reticence and have attempted to demonstrate to them that they have a remarkable, novel opportunity to create an atmosphere of loving closeness with their children if they discuss this with them. If a father discusses sex with his son, he can use the opportunity to develop a more caring relationship, one in which there is burgeoning empathy between parent and child based on a mutual recognition that the feelings discussed will be felt by both even though at the time they may be felt by only one. But think of the opportunities for empathy and closeness if a father sits down with a daughter and discusses the changes going on in her body, pointing out that he can understand and appreciate those changes even though he cannot share them biologically. I remember one father coming to see me after having gone to the drug store with his 11-year-old daughter to show her how to buy sanitary napkins, and telling me that he does not think anything will ever drive them apart after passing through that cauldron (the term was his) together.

Mothers, too, can discuss sex with their sons. They should, in fact, because they can probably teach them even better the necessity for gentleness and consideration associated with sexual feelings. Talking about the feelings, in fact, is the greatest stumbling block in these discussions regardless of who does the discussing. Most parents of either sex, single or married, can discuss biology to some extent. Even more *can* discuss feelings, but they are embarassed. It may be necessary to teach the mechanics and biology of menstruation and erection and orgasm, but it is even more necessary for parents to teach children about the kinds of feelings which emerge when confronted with a desirable creature of the opposite sex.

In my experience, single parents of both sexes can provide that marvelous and intensely needed knowledge for their children of both sexes, and they must. The lack of embarassment in dealing with this will cause the child to perceive his or her parent as a person to whom he or she can bring anything for discussion, a trait which will be increasingly valuable as the children pass through adolescence and beyond.

Breaking up the household does not necessitate a lack of closeness between child and parent. If anything, it mandates increased closeness, and the opportunity to develop that closeness by discussing sex and its associated feelings ought not to be sacrificed. That is real quality time—and it lasts.

————— · —————

These questions are directed to all separated or divorced parents:

- Where did you learn about sex? How accurate was your learning?
- Did anyone ever talk with you about sexual feelings as distinct from sexual biology? Do you think that was or would have been helpful?
- Did your parent of the opposite sex ever discuss any of this with you?

  — How did you, or would you, have felt?
  — If you felt discomfort, what was its source? Was your parent uncomfortable?
  — In the eyes of your parent, was sex a good thing?
  — Is it a good thing in your own eyes?
  — If it is not, do you want to get that message across to your children? (Be honest, now.)

- How will you get lessons across about restraint and morality in the face of your positive expressions about sex? Further, how can you get that message across if they know that you are engaging in a sexual relationship out of marriage?

CHAPTER 8

. . .

Out of My Files

Raising children is hard work. Forgive me, please, Dr. Spock, but it's really true. Oh sure, it's rewarding more than anything else I can imagine, but the rewards come between the agonies. Probably most parents will agree with that statement whether they are married or divorced. Although it may be harder to rear kids after a divorce, the baseline is difficult to begin with. A number of divorced parents I have seen in my practice appear to have forgotten this point. They often come to me and complain about the problems they are having with their children, but when I question them carefully about their history and especially about problems which might have existed before the divorce or even before the trouble began brewing between the spouses, it often emerges that troubles are not new to those children.

Children who are troubled before a divorce are likely to be more troubled after a divorce. The adaptation and adjustment patterns of children may be made more difficult following a family breakup, but those children who have manifested such problems as school or learning difficulties, hyperactivity or overaggressivity, problems with socialization with peers, or bedwetting are at special risk following a divorce. Children whose adaptation patterns have been, by and large, within normal or expected limits will probably adjust better to the divorce—given the benefits of time and the blessings of parents who will not fight over them and pull them apart.

———— . ————

As I listen to my patients, often I begin to recognize a pattern of concern common to many of them. The guilt feelings of the divorced parents are often such that they feel that everything which happens to the children is a product of the divorce. Frequently they use that as an opportunity to damn the ex-spouse either for leaving or for doing bad things to the children during visitation. They look at their own roles less often, usually only with help. Generally only with help can they learn that their own anxieties may be transmitted to the kids who then develop behavioral or adjustment problems.

Sometimes I am able to assure the parents that the problems of the child are not due to the divorce at all. Divorce is certainly bad for kids, but it is not the cause of every problem which may develop in the children of divorce. The kids live in an increasingly complex world, and many other people and stimuli cause them to react and respond in many and varied ways.

———— . ————

The first rule, therefore, is to take a good, deep breath before automatically blaming the divorce for what is happening to your children. Determine whether the kids are really responding to something else which is bothering them. If you feel strongly that the problem really is the divorce, take another deep breath before you start to blame your ex-spouse. Look at your own relationship with the children first. Only after that can you blame someone else.

———— . ————

It's Only Money

Finances are tight in the 1980s, and they will stay that way for some time to come. Job security is not at the safe level it used to be, automation is rearing its remarkable head, and all this is occurring during a time of continuing, if slowed, inflation and a shortage of spendable income. Two-household families, the inevitable result of divorce, always suffer economically. It is, indeed, easier to feed and house an intact family than a split one.

The children continue to be bombarded by the media which advertise all kinds of good things for them, but the financial straits of the family prevent the purchase of all the new toys they see on television. That happens in many intact families, too. Single women who are rearing their children feel this more acutely than single fathers, usually because their salaries are generally less than those of their ex-husbands because they have generally been out of the labor force for a while and have little experience. They usually start lower on the economic ladder.

Single mothers often complain about their financial stresses, not so much for their own sakes as for the sakes of the children. A good example is the vacation trauma. School is out during the summer, and all the other kids (as described by your own children) are going to all sorts of marvelous places. Why can't we? Why are we always broke? Why can everybody else do it? I shall only briefly mention the obvious—the complaints the mothers make are really not as much for the sake of the kids as for the mothers' own sakes. Strapped mothers identify with their strapped kids. They feel deprivation as much if not more than the children.

It is no crime to identify with the needs of your children. It is no crime to want to do more for them and for yourself and to feel badly that you cannot. It ought to be a crime, though, to ignore the possibilities of doing some things which are not that costly and which can provide you and your children with a good time. You are all entitled to it. Saving for a holiday is a worthy cause. Vacations do not have to mean transcontinental flights to exotic or expensive locales. Camping at state parks is genuine fun. Intact families do it, why can't divorced households? Why can't divorced parents team up with their friends, other divorced parents, and pool their vacation savings? Pooled savings mean that you can go a lot better and a lot farther.

The benefits of a trip together are remarkable. I recall one patient who was the mother of two adolescent sons. The father had long since withdrawn from the family. She became anxious and depressed over the demands of rearing her boys, and this led to the symptoms which brought her to see me. As it turned out, she was really doing better with the kids than she feared. They were limit testers, as are most adolescents, but she did not feel secure in her ability to maintain the limits beyond which they would not pass. She never considered that they actually had never stepped over the line with her.

A little emotional support went a long way with her, until the guilt over vacation time appeared. She and her two sons had never been camping before. Neither boy had any scouting experience. The mother consulted with a neighbor who was an experienced camper, and she borrowed just a little of their equipment after learning how to use it correctly. The three of them went off in their beat-up station wagon to a nearby state park for a practice session. The stories I heard on the mother's return were worthy of *I Love Lucy,* but they went again and then again to a park a little farther away. After a time, she really did not need to see a therapist anymore, so we terminated our therapeutic relationship, but the next summer I received a postcard from Yosemite, with a message indicating that they were now confirmed and enthusiastic campers.

I am not touting camping specifically. I must confess that I am not even fond of it, personally, although I would be the last to put it down as a superb opportunity for families to get together on better terms. What I am touting is an attempt to do something together which takes you away from home and brings you into a new environment which you can share together. If you are able to set aside a larger sum which will allow a more elaborate or a longer trip, you will never regret the opportunity it will provide you. It will not be wasted money.

The wishes of the children are important here. Their choices of vacation spots—within reason—must be solicited and respected. Planning provides good times, too. If they come up with a practical idea, follow through with it. Travel agents can be very helpful, even to single mothers. If they are sexists, they will want your business if you remarry and get a wealthy new husband or, if they are realists, when you get that longed-for promotion at work.

Vacation experiences can provide real quality time, and they also provide nostalgic reminiscences for long times to come. The children will appreciate the attempts you make as a single parent. That, too, will draw you closer.

——— · ———

These questions are directed to all separated or divorced parents:

- What do *you* like to do for recreation?
- Do you think you can get your children to enjoy those same activities and to want to share them with you?

    — Do *you* want to share them?
    — Are they really suitable for children?
    — Are the children still too young?
    — If so, what will you do?

A Chip Off the Old Block

Parents sometimes complain that they are unable to develop the requisite warmth and good feelings they know they should have toward one or all of their children. When I hear this from divorced parents, I automatically begin to question the complainer about the ex-spouse, because my experience is that the problem child often looks or acts like the ex-spouse, and the custodial parent cannot tolerate that. When I hear the same complaint from a parent in an intact household, I begin to ask questions about his or her parents. The same dynamic appears. Whenever there are problems causing rejection by the parents of young children, one should wonder just what or whom the parent sees in that child which causes such distancing. If the rejecting parent sees the hated ex-spouse or the hated parent in the face of the child, that child is going to receive lots of displaced anger from the parent.

In psychotherapy, it is not difficult to establish the presence of this dynamic. It is necessary to teach the complaining parent that he or she may be entitled to be angry at the child for what the child does, but that the anger must be proportional to the deed. Often the parents overreact, letting out a whole wellspring of anger centering about the ex-spouse and really directed toward him or her. The amount of anger expressed is far too great for the stimulus and probably has nothing to do with the child's behavior.

Divorced parents are very sensitive to behavior which reminds them of their ex-spouses. Because of their sensitivity, they will overreact to the behavior itself, in a manner which not only allows the wellspring of inappropriate rage to emerge but also creates a reservoir of fear within themselves. Those fearful parents will tell themselves something like "Oh, my god! He's going to grow up to be just like his father!"

Single mothers have no monopoly on this behavior. I have heard single fathers complain about their daughters whose blonde hair reminds them of their ex-spouse, and I especially recall one case where a father complained about his son because he looked like his mother. The father was terrified that this meant that the boy was going to grow up to be a homosexual! That is one of the very few cases in which I thought seriously about recommending a change in custody for the child, even though there was no lawsuit asking for a change. That father was seriously emotionally ill and could provide little for the increasingly anxious little boy, but there was no viable placement alternative. Fortunately, the father began to respond to treatment, and the child's anxiety began to wane.

A related topic centers about the issue of the child's wishes to look like the parent who is not in the home. One father went through the roof when his preteen-aged daughter began combing her hair in a way taught her by her mother whom she had visited and whom she wanted to emulate. Eventually, he was able to see that it was appropriate for his daughter to identify with her own mother and that, even though he hated the woman, he never hated her looks.

Another episode was stimulated by the child's insistence on keeping a picture of his father on his dresser in his room. The mother, only recently divorced, became very upset whenever she saw it. Her own defensiveness was marked, and she began to fear that the boy loved her less than he did the father. It was very difficult to get her to see that the child loved and needed both of them and that it was a comfort to the child to have a picture of the longed-for father near him. After a time she was able to appreciate the fact that a comforted child is a child whose adjustment will be smoother and easier. Again, the record shows that providing the child with the necessary access to both parents makes life much easier for children and parents.

———— . ————

The following questions are directed to all separated or divorced parents:

• Do you somehow feel differently toward the child who looks or acts like you?

— Do you feel closer toward him or her?
— Do you distance yourself from that child?
— What do you think that means? About the child? About yourself?

• Does your family ever comment in the child's presence that he or she is a picture of you or of your former spouse?

— How do you feel about those comments?
— How do you feel about the resemblances?
— How do you feel about the child?

Ho, Ho, Ho! It's Holiday Time!

It is a psychiatric cliché that major holidays are the most depressing times of the year. Perhaps Christmas is the outstanding example, not just because of the extraordinary length of time spent preparing for it, but also because it evokes in all of us images of family-oriented childhoods. Even Scrooge became a family man after a fashion, adopting Tiny Tim and the whole Cratchit brood. That made him happy. At Christmas time, we always seem to ask ourselves if *we* are happy. When we have grown up and have lost our parents or other beloved family members, all the stimuli of Christmas cause us pain, because they do nothing but remind us of our losses.

When custody agreements are signed, even without battles, expectations regarding visitation are usually spelled out. Holidays figure importantly in those expectations. The custodial parent probably has the children through the school year except for weekends or occasional week nights, but when the summer holidays or the Christmas holidays come around, the visiting parent has more of an opportunity to spend more time with the children. So often anger results from those times: The custodial parent resents giving up the child for times longer than a weekend and especially resents giving up the child over holidays which then leave him or her lonelier than otherwise. Again, we see the parent depending on the child for companionship and emotional support, just as described in an earlier chapter.

Holidays are also hard on the visiting parent and perhaps even harder on his or her new spouse. Consider the possibility that the stepparent has children of her or his own. They may live with them, or they, too, may visit. The adaptation of a family to the introduction of two disparate groups of children provides a real test of ability.

If both divorced parents live in the same community, are there problems about attending the usual school holiday programs? Why should there be? There ought to be enough seats in the auditorium for everybody and certainly enough to place the divorced parents far enough apart.

If the parents live in different communities, are there fights over who pays for the transportation? Weren't these details worked out in the original custody and visitation agreement?

Do the grandparents expect or subtly demand time which takes the children away from either or both parents? Can't time be arranged to share the children instead of stretching them apart?

Which is the most important time, Christmas eve or Christmas morning? The most important time is the time when the children are with you. It is a sad commentary that the most important time is usually present-opening time, even in intact families. But that offers an opportunity. The kids can open their presents either time or both times.

Is it any wonder that Christmas is often so depressing? It ought not to be made depressing for visiting children by either parent. Making sure that the holiday visit goes well is a terrific Christmas present.

Birthdays are also holidays for children, perhaps even more meaningful to them than Christmas. What is the attitude of the custodial parent when a present arrives from the parent who is out of the home? Can that parent come to give the present in person? What should the custodial parent's attitude be?

———— · ————

Attitude is all-important here. Anticipation of a holiday or a special event can be an exciting pleasure or it can be an anxious drag. If only problems are expected, they will result. Both custodial and visiting parents must develop the capacity to work together at least enough to make these occasions positively worthwhile for the children. As parents, you will be rewarded by doing so. Life will be much easier, and you will be able to find the reserve strength to make the holidays better for yourselves, too.

———— · ————

Not-So-Evil Stepparents

The new mates of the divorced spouses are always the fall guys in postdivorce relationships. Resentment toward them by the spouse left behind is usually enormous, and the new mates are often blamed for the divorce even if they did not meet the ex-spouses until long after the separation. Feelings such as these can certainly affect the children who are to visit with the separated parent and new spouse.

The mythology surrounding stepparents is vast, and it is usually colored by the same fears and resentments I just de-scribed. In ages past, even greater resentment was socially expected because of the rarity of divorce. In cases of the death of a parent and his or her replacement by another mate, the feelings of abandonment felt by the child when the parent died provided the basis for the writers of fairy tales to scare us all. Cinderella is mild—at least she gets her prince.

Mythology is hard to overcome. The expectation that a stepparent is going to be a tough hurdle for a child often sets up a problem situation where one need not exist. Does the child begin to develop the fear by himself or herself, or does the fear operate via suggestion from the other parent? I have talked with a number of children about their stepparents and about their expectations of how they would be. Most told us that they really had very little problem with the stepparent. They had more problems with the stepparent's spouse—the biological parent.

Most of the children have told me that the stepparent in the home of the noncustodial parent is a considerate and loving person and that the stepparent often does most of the caretaking when the child visits. I speak here mainly of stepmothers, but the same can be said of stepfathers when the children come to visit. Most of the children told me that their stepparents were better than the stepparents of most of their friends. I always wonder if their friends would tell me the same thing.

My experience has been that stepfathers and stepmothers in the households of the noncustodial parents do well with the children. The visits usually go well. Where problems exist, they usually occur in the custodial households where the stepparents live all the time with the children, but even then, more often than not, the stepparents are nowhere near the ferocious ogres painted by the Brothers Grimm and their ilk. Some may be immature or difficult in other ways, but those difficulties are not specifically centered about the children or even directed primarily at them. The personality problems certainly may spill over into their relationships with the children, or in their avoidance of those relationships. But these days, with the proliferation of divorce, more and more stepparents are entering situations prepared to function in those roles. The children are more sophisticated, too, even at young ages. Often, they expect little from their stepparents, and they adopt a live-and-let-live attitude with them, saving questions, requests, and similar favors for the real parents. That presents a sometimes shaky family equilibrium, but it may work well, especially if the stepparent does not become too defensive about it. The wise biological parent will try to steer the child *slowly* into a more accepting and open relationship with the stepparent.

Biological parents who remarry and find that their new mates are antagonistic or otherwise rejecting toward their children living with them must assume the responsibility for and do something about the situation. Some questions to ask include: What was the attitude of the new mate before he or she moved in? Before they married? Could the hostility have been predicted? Was it apparent, and, if so, why did the relationship proceed?

What role should the new stepparent assume in the household? Obviously, the role differs according to sex and according to the ages and needs of the children. Most important, the role depends on the latitude provided by the real parent and by the agreements made between real parent and stepparent before marriage.

When a stepparent lives in the same household on an ongoing basis with the children, and the children are young and the divorced parent has withdrawn from the family, the stepparent will find it much easier to assume the parental role. It is tragic that such relative ease partially results from the fact that the other parent is no longer around. Even in such an instance, the wise stepparent will build a relationship slowly with the children, using the children's responses as a good guide to how fast it should develop or how authoritative the relationship should be.

In any event, a stepfather should not automatically become a stereotyped disciplinarian. In fact, neither should a step-mother. Both should proceed slowly, recognizing that a great deal of provocative behavior by the children may be the result of their resentment of the stepparent's very presence. Where most stepparents make mistakes is in their rushed approach to taking over. They become defensive and anxious in their attempts to maintain their new position at the top of the family pyramid. They also make a serious mistake if they attempt to change families according to their own ideas of what families should be, regardless of the ways the children were brought up before the stepparent appeared on the scene. Wise stepparents and their spouses will recognize that they are not rebuilding a nuclear family. It is a reconstituted family. As with oil and water, some good emulsifiers may be needed to make a working, effective blend.

The best emulsifier is maturity. They must be sufficiently sound and secure so that they do not compete with the children for the spouse. Everyone loses in family power struggles. The children cannot be expected to know that, so the parents and stepparents will have to prevent them for everybody's sake. When the stepparent lives with the children whose divorced parent still sees them, there is an automatically different function and relationship. The stepparent may perform a number of parental duties and have a number of parental obligations, but when both other parents are still in the picture, the stepparent is left without as much authority or acceptance as he or she might need. This may cause trouble.

The role of the biological parent then becomes increasingly crucial. He or she needs maturity, too. The real parent serves as the conduit between the children and the stepparent, always encouraging both in the formation of a close and understanding relationship. The biological parent must also understand the child's fears that the stepparent will take the parent away, that the stepparent caused the divorce, or that the stepparent will be like those in the fairy tales. It is important that the biological parent and the children share time together without the stepparent, especially at first and probably less later if the stepparent develops a close, accepted relationship with the children.

In stepparent families, it is very important that the parent figures have time together both for their own sakes and so that they can talk about the children. Only by doing that can they establish a common and mutually consistent approach with them. In intact families, children often try to split the parents to gain their own ends. In stepparents' families, children may find it easier to do if parents make no concerted effort to avoid it. If the children succeed, the situation becomes harder in the long run, for them as well as for their parents.

What about the parent who is left behind? That parent is often the crux of the problems which develop when the other spouse remarries. If the new stepparent is ideal—free, easy, open, and loving—and if the child longs to develop a solid relationship with him or her, how much does the other parent cause the child to hold back? Again, loyalty conflicts may be generated. What is the response of the parent left behind when the child comes back and tells delightful stories about the new stepparent?

In my experience, the concept of children as property plays a significant role here. As an example, the parent left behind fears losing the child to the new family. That parent is so fearful and defensive that he or she cannot perceive that the child remains as close and as loving as always and that the child would be terrified if there would ever be a rupture with that parent. If child-oriented, that parent would encourage a good relationship with the new stepparent because it would benefit the child. But all the real parent in such a case has to hear is the child referring in parental terms to the new stepparent, such as "Daddy," or, "Mommy," and the world begins to cave in.

The parent fails to see that the child's needs for reassurance and stability are being placated and filled by the new relationship. The parent fails to see that such a relationship benefits the parent if it benefits the child. Instead, all that parent can feel is threatened by the potential loss of the child, just as he or she previously lost the ex-spouse. The danger of a self-fulfilling prophecy emerges in this situation. If a loss is feared so much, a loss may be stimulated and provoked by the parent's rejection of the child. Everybody loses in a situation where everybody could gain so very much.

——— · ———

These questions are for all separated or divorced parents:

• After breaking up with your spouse, why are you in such a hurry to force a relationship between your children and your new significant other?

— Do you rationalize, "They're going to have to accept the fact eventually that I'm going to be with him/her?"
— How frustrated do you get when the children do not accept him/her?
— How do you respond? Do you back off or push harder?
— Does pushing harder ever get you anywhere?
— Do you really want that relationship between your new mate and the children to bloom as soon as possible so that you can feel less guilty about it?

Different Directions

I am still surprised when patients tell me that they are surprised that their ex-spouses are applying different methods, standards, values and goals to their tasks of rearing the children. For example, sometimes a mother comes in and complains that the children's father is teaching them bad habits. Frequent examples of these include laziness and a disrespect for organization and responsibility (remember always, a perception of lack of structure might only mean that there is a different structure). The complaints usually begin with a tale of slovenly behavior by the children after returning home from a visit to the father. The mothers (usually the more overtly organized and structured parents and more often than not the custodial parents) then express resentment toward their ex-husbands for making them into nags in the eyes of the kids. They perceive themselves as being seen as the "bad guys" and the fathers as the "good guys" because of their laxness, creating more hard feelings.

These mothers (or sometimes fathers, if they are the more organized or custodial parents) need time to breathe a little easier about that situation and to recognize that the children really do not perceive them in as bad a light as they begin to perceive themselves. Once again, parental guilt strikes home. The children can press the guilt-inducing buttons easily in those parents who begin to see themselves as harsh. After all, they reason, why should they make life harder on their poor, fatherless (motherless) children by nagging or having heartless expectations of better performance?

The answer to that query is simple and positive. The children need them to maintain their standards. They need the custodial parent to uphold values and to be consistent; children, in their anxiety about the breakup of the household, fear that the remaining parent will break up, too. Not falling for guilt-provoking charges by the children and, even more, not falling for the parent's own guilt-provoking impressions of being made into the bad guy by the opposing spouse will ease the anxiety of both child and parent.

Also, the differences between ex-spouses may be real, not manufactured for manipulative purposes. They may be fundamental in terms of their approaches to life and to child rearing. Certainly, they had differences enough to cause their marriage to fail. That's why I am automatically surprised when divorced parents complain about the different approaches used by their ex-spouses, as if they are unaware that they should expect differences.

Often I hear one parent describe his or her ex-spouse's pushing the children too hard toward a goal which is really not the children's goal but the other parent's goal. Examples of this include excellence at school or in other organized activities. Sometimes the children actually become upset if they are not able to please the pushing parent by getting high grades, by getting into the best school, or by becoming accomplished in sports or music or whatever. Sometimes the pushing parent wants the children to become social lions or lionesses early. Sometimes the parent pushes premature dating or opposite-sex contacts. This can stimulate anxiety in kids who may not be ready.

Here is where the other parent serves a very helpful purpose by supporting the child as much as possible. If the pushing parent is really expressing his or her personality by pushing, little can be done about this, and attempts to limit the custody or visitation with that parent usually only create greater problems. Besides, more often than not, experience shows that pushing parents can demonstrate excellent reasoning powers which serve them well in court if the case gets carried that far—which it usually should not.

The supportive parent must recognize with the child that the child is being pushed by the other parent and must also acknowledge that the situation may not be fair or even reasonable. A good shoulder to cry on is always welcome and is an appropriate offering of a parent. Supportive parents must also teach their children that they will simply have to do the best they can even if other parents' goals are unrealistic. Children must eventually learn that they will have to deal with a number of unrealistic people in this world, but they will learn better and more easily if someone close assures them that they will be loved.

Supportive parents will need to emphasize to the children that their other parent loves them and that he or she only wants the best from them and for them. Generally, this is a true statement, even if the pushing parent is acting out his or her own feelings of inadequacy by getting the kids to do things inappropriately. The supportive parent must also promise to remain close to the children and to help them as much as possible, easing the burden as much as possible although unable to eliminate it completely.

If the supportive parent is the visiting parent, much of the visiting time will be spent by the child complaining about the unreasonable expectations of the custodial parent. The temptation may be great to sue for custody then, but this should generally be resisted. The temptation to place an arm around the child's shoulder or to give him or her a hug should not be resisted. Sometimes the supportive parent does the best job by simply being around to pick up the pieces. Picking up the pieces is quality time.

———— · ————

The following questions are for all separated or divorced parents:

- How much do you *really* believe that different people can have different beliefs and approaches to life and still be good, fruitful, and worthwhile?

  — Why are you so upset that your kids are learning different approaches or values from their other parent?
  — Are those approaches and values really bad, or are they only threatening to you because they are different?
  — If you and your ex-spouse had stuck together, would the children have been exposed to those same values anyway?

- How do you deal with those differences? Can you be open enough with the kids to teach them that they can behave one way in one place (as long as the behavior is not antisocial) and another way in a different place when the people in those different places expect different things from them? Can you teach them the valuable lesson of determining the expectations of the people with them?

CHAPTER 9

— . . . —

What the Children Must Do

Throughout this book, I have written instructions for parents and stepparents in the hope that their children will benefit from them and receive the quality time they deserve. If consistent quality time results from the relationships established and maintained with parents and stepparents following divorce, the children will probably do well. They will probably still have problems because their family is no longer intact and because they feel rejected by one or both parents, but time, patience, openness, and honesty on the parts of *all* parent figures—custodial parents, visiting parents, and stepparents—will help a great deal.

Children also have a lot of emotional work to do after their parents divorce. They must do that work to reconstitute their lives and proceed into relatively untroubled adulthood. Dr.

Judith Wallerstein has performed and directed an enormous amount of research about the children of divorce in her capacity as the director of the Center for the Study of Families in Transition, in Marin County, California. It is appropriate to conclude this book with a summary of her findings regarding the six essential psychological tasks which children of divorce must perform if they are to rid themselves of the most problematic aftereffects of the family breakup.

The period of disorganization in the children of divorce may last several years or longer if they are in troubled and continually conflicted families. Only after that time in some families can there be any expectation that stability will reach a reasonable level so that the child can begin to work on these tasks. Wallerstein has described them as a sequence of stages or events, but, as with all processes of growth and development, they usually overlap. It takes years to go through them successfully. Chronic litigation over custody or visitation or chronic quarreling over the children without actually filing lawsuits will only lengthen the time before the children can settle down and get to work. If they have already started, those kinds of problems will only toss a monkey wrench into the process. You have to help them. In so doing, you will help yourself.

——— · ———

Remember, the children must accomplish these tasks, not the parents, but the children cannot be expected to perform them without the requisite degree of love, encouragement, and family stability which can only be provided by parents who provide ongoing and real quality time for them.

——— · ———

Task 1: Acknowledging the Reality of the Marital Rupture

I pointed out earlier that children fantasize that their families are going to reconstitute and that the missing parent will return so that the family will go on uninterrupted. Children have a nearly impossible time giving up that hope. I frequently become aware of the persistence of that fantasy in many of my adult patients who continue to cling to it after many years and after any reasonable or logical thought might be expected to set it aside. Reason and logic have very little to do with the governance of our affairs. Feelings are at the base of most of our responses and our behaviors.

How can you help your child to give up this fantasy? First, you must recognize that the child clings to it out of fear. To a child, the intact family is the only buffering agent against the world. The breadwinner and the caretaker worked as a team, clothing and feeding the child and determining activities, standards, and expectations. Without an intact team, what can the child expect? After all, what does he or she know about the world and how to deal with it? That lack of knowledge stimulates other fantasies as well—destructive and fearsome fantasies based on the lack of consistent support provided by the intact household. Those fantasies, too, linger for long times.

Reassurance is essential here. Verbal assurance is fine, but the child's fear will probably not allow him or her to believe the message initially. The child will have even more trouble taking the reassuring parent's word if that parent does not follow through.

The children must be told that the parent who left is not going to come back to rejoin the family, but that he or she still loves the children and will continue to see them. The children, like us, can only hope that promise will be kept.

It is always best if the leaving parent talks to the child. That parent will need to deal with the child's spoken or unspoken expectation that the parent may be leaving because of the child and that the parent no longer loves the child. The leaving parent will have to explain that not loving the other parent any more does not mean that the child is not loved, explaining that adults may fall out of love but that parents and children cannot fall out of love. Most important, the leaving parent must *demonstrate* that fact to the child, repeatedly, regularly, religiously, and over a prolonged period of time. Only then will the child begin to believe it.

Maybe, the child is told, the parent will not see the child in the child's home. Maybe the parent will see the child elsewhere, perhaps in a new home that the parent will establish. But, in any event, the child is going to remain safe and happy in this home (or with the parent with whom the child stays, if the family will be moving) and will continue to be loved and cared for by both.

For years the child will fantasize or dream about parental reconciliation, long after stepparents enter the scene and long after any reasonable hope is dashed. Parents must expect that they will be bothered by any emerging comments from the children indicating that they cling to these hopes. The parents will also notice that the children are more nervous and overtly anxious, and this will bother them, too. The children may overreact to stimuli, developing what psychiatrists call *increased startle reactions*. The children remain scared until they are sure in their own minds that they do not have to be scared any longer. Ordinarily, that takes a long time.

To be less bothered by the children's symptoms, the parents must understand them better. To be less bothered themselves, the children must understand better the reality that they will continue to be cared for. The parents must work with them to get the children to believe this, slowly, patiently, and with constant confirmation of their love.

———— · ————

Task 2: Disengaging from Interparent Conflicts and Resuming Customary Pursuits

Earlier, I discussed the necessity that parents continue to function in the eye of a tornado. Children also will need to function there, and for them it is even harder.

Growth requires consistent and continuing giving to the child by the parent, not of material things but of concern and care. A good definition of growth is that it is the outcome of a series of carefully controlled and selected frustrations. The level of the child's frustration must be carefully controlled by the parent, who must determine whether the child can accomplish a given task. The parent must also determine whether the child's response to being unable to complete the task successfully is too upsetting. If so, a slightly easier task may result in either success or better-tolerated disappointment.

For example, children should be expected to collect trash before they are expected to do the dishes. Crawling comes before walking and walking before running. Realistic expectations should always be combined with support by the parent and praise for success.

Failures can be overcome and conquered, providing children with a sense of security with which they tackle the next carefully selected hurdle. Nothing succeeds like success!

Selection of the hurdles is a delicate and careful task. Needy parents find it harder to do this, and nowhere are parents needier than in the eye of the tornado of divorce. The development of individual identities in children may be set back considerably by the dissension in the separated or newly divorced household. That stress is not a carefully selected frustration, and that hurdle may just be too much.

The children may cling to the parent who remains. They may regress into earlier and more primitive developmental stages. Old patterns of behavior, such as bedwetting or soiling, babytalk, sleep disturbances, or whiney clinging may make the situation worse by exasperating an already stressed parent.

These phases are not restricted to very young children. They affect children of all ages. Characteristically, we see the development of delinquent activities in adolescent children of divorce, who, disgusted with their own household and able to express their disgust and hurt only by acting it out against the world, thereby get back at the parents. Theft is probably the most common activity for delinquent adolescents here. The symbolic nature of taking something they want does not require a psychiatrist to interpret.

Younger children also have problems in continuing their customary pursuits. School is the most significant and active of their customary pursuits, and school problems abound during this stage. Failures there serve only to lower an already-lowered sense of self-esteem. Peer relationships may suffer because of that lowered sense of self-esteem. The children often develop feelings of shame or of being "different" because of the divorce even if they recognize that many of their friends come from divorced households. Kids need encouragement during this stage, a rare commodity when the parents are disorganized and discouraged themselves.

Task 3: Resolving Loss

What is definitely lost is the intact household. What may be lost over and above that is the absent parent.

Routine changes in a separated household. Children are accustomed to routine, and they find changes in it difficult to cope with. The loss of routine provokes anxiety, and the loss of status (as a new child of divorce) and all the other losses create depression. Depression results from losses of things personally significant to the patient. Material things can be lost, and we can all get depressed for short times when depressing events occur. But when children face a whole series of losses of such severe significance, it is to be expected that they will become clinically depressed. Clinical depressions are deeper and last longer than the blues we all get at times.

Peace must be made with the fact that things are no longer the same and that they will not return to what used to be normal. It often takes a lot of crying before peace is made. The children cry and the parents cry—with each other and separately.

What helps most is the reestablishment of the relationships between parents and the children. Certainly, consistent and steady visitation by the absent parent is essential, and the presence of the custodial parent is always reassuring if the custodial parent is able to deal with his or her own problems. Smooth joint custody, if possible, can help very much during this stage.

Here is where a good, patient stepparent can provide a great service to the child. Recognition by the stepparent that the child needs what the stepparent can offer but that the child is afraid of having to give up the absent parent to accept it may help the stepparent to get closer.

Task 4: Resolving Anger and Self-Blame

This stage probably persists longer than any of the others. Kids stay mad longer, often through their adult lives. This anger often forms the basis of the need for adults to see therapists because of their inabilities to develop happy interpersonal relationships.

Remember the cries of infants? When they are frustrated, whether because of hunger, wet pants, pain, or whatever, they cry *loudly*. They sound angry when they cry because they are angry. Anger is the fundamental emotion of frustration. Only as they develop do infants begin to make recognizably specific cries which mothers and fathers can identify.

The anger that children feel is akin to that basic anger

expressed by infants. In every sense, the children feel as helpless and every bit as frustrated. In fact, if they are older, they
are probably angrier. The separation of their parents and the
breaking up of their home is the most severe blow they have
ever suffered. Their anger may make it difficult for even the
most hard-working and earnest parent to reach the children.
The kids may be too angry to listen or to want to talk.

Good friends, neighbors, teachers, ministers, doctors—all
are worthy helpers here. It is urgent to get the children to talk.
To whom they talk makes little difference as long as the listener
is an understanding adult in fair control of his or her own
emotions. Talking long and loud and hard about the separation is a good way to defuse the resentment. If talking with an
outsider helps the child talk with the parents, so much the
better.

Children who blame themselves are very common in divorce situations. This is related to the anger they feel. That
anger has nowhere to go. Even if it is expressed to the parents,
the parents will not do what the child wants—they will not
reconcile. The rage becomes impotent, and children turn it
against themselves. They feel even guiltier and more self-blam-
ing than before.

Talking is essential for that, too. Parents need to understand these dynamics so that they can help their children get
through this awful stage. As the children get older and, it is
hoped, increasingly mature, they will be better able to deal with
these feelings and will make peace with the anger just as they
made peace with the earlier feelings of loss.

Task 5: Accepting the Permanence
of the Divorce

Obviously, this is related to the first of the tasks, that of
acknowledging the reality of the marital rupture. Because the
child usually prolongs the wishes and fantasies regarding rec-

onciliation and family restitution, Wallerstein has emphasized that process by calling attention to the separate, later portion of that stage.

Sometimes a child will acknowledge the rupture without accepting that it is permanent. The avoidance of that last acceptance is a gimmick. It allows the child to maintain the reconciliation fantasy, if not consciously and as overtly as before, then at least unconsciously and covertly. It is hard for children to give up their homes. It is even harder for them to give up their fantasies, because the giving-up process depends on them.

Again, reassurance is the answer, combined with consistent love and the ability to maintain continued closeness with both parents. Both parents should continue to emphasize to the children that they will not get together again, but that they will not give the children up.

Task 6: Achieving Realistic Hopes Regarding Relationships

In my practice I see so many people who have been emotionally burned by poor relationships or broken relationships. These patients have been crushed by the harsh disappointment resulting from the loss of those emotional investments, and they have become wary of engaging in the hunt for replacement relationships. They run grave dangers of being very lonely and depressed old people long before their time.

Children are even more susceptible to being burned emotionally. When they have grown up in an atmosphere of hostility and parental acting-out one against the other, they develop a skewed outlook. Their version of the world is a hostile and unrewarding place, inevitably made worse by disappointments in loving relationships. They know little and learn less about positive relationships. They may have no role models to provide them with that kind of framework (unless they have allowed themselves to view objectively a lucky marriage by the custodial parent to a good stepparent). What kind of future do those children of divorce have?

Obviously, they have very poor chances for marital happiness if they do not know anything about how to achieve it. They may say that their earlier experiences have taught them how *not* to relate to a potential or actual mate, but they never learned how to do the actual relating.

For a child of divorce to be able to determine realistically that there may be chances for good and lasting, loving relationships in this world, he or she will have had to progress through all of the previous phases of adaptation to the divorce. That takes a fair number of years, and usually the whole task is characterized by a few steps backward interspersed with the forward ones. Even when those previous five stages have been completed successfully, danger still lurks; the failure of one significant relationship in adulthood will allow the suppressed fear of inevitable inadequacy to come to the fore. The new adult will say to himself or herself, "You see? I told you so!" and effectively block the development of further relationships. It is hard to convince those people that it is unusual, sometimes even necessary to proceed through a series of relationships before the definite, right relationship is found. They are too attuned to longing, seeking passionately, finding, and validating their preexisting thesis that a relationship won't work.

Often, these people actually provoke problems in relationships to validate their underlying prediction. They are unaware of doing that, just as they may be unaware that they have that underlying need to prove that relationships just do not work in life. If they can prove that all relationships fail, they can make peace with their parents' failures more easily. They can rationalize that their parents' marriage was doomed because all marriages are doomed. Throughout their lives they long to be less angry with their parents for their divorces, and they play these kinds of mental tricks on themselves to achieve that goal.

Making that peace may make them less rageful toward their parents, but it does not really help them very much. Parents must teach their children that it is never necessary for the kids to be so much like them that they repeat their mistakes.

——— . ———

Quality time spent with children is the goal of every thinking, realistic, practical divorced parent. When divorced parents can provide that consistently for their children, they are working constructively with the children toward the ultimate progression through these six necessary tasks. The tasks are not easy for the children. After all, they have to start after receiving the blow of the divorce! They have to get up off the floor and come back for the next six rounds.

What is remarkable is that so many can do that. When they do, their triumphs represent testimonials to the efforts of their parents and stepparents. Those efforts really pay off. They pay off for the children, and they pay off for the parents. Take my word for it: I've seen sick kids and I've seen happy kids. Happy is better.

Index